AMERICA'S
PURPOSE

AMERICA'S PURPOSE

New Visions
of U.S. Foreign Policy

EDITED BY

Owen Harries

OF

The National Interest

ICS PRESS

ICS

San Francisco, California

Printed in the United States on acid-free paper by ICS Press. All rights reserved. The chapters in this book were previously published in *The National Interest*. No part of this book may be used or reproduced in any manner without written permission except in the case of brief quotations in critical articles and reviews. Reprint permission and duplication requests should be addressed to *The National Interest*, 1112 Sixteenth Street, NW, Suite 540, Washington, DC 20036.

Inquiries, book orders, and catalog requests should be addressed to ICS Press, 243 Kearny Street, San Francisco, CA 94108. (415) 981-5353. Fax (415) 986-4878. To order call toll-free (800) 326-0263 in the contiguous United States. Distributed to the trade by National Book Network.

The Institute for Contemporary Studies is a nonpartisan, non-profit public policy research organization. The analyses, conclusions, and opinions in ICS Press publications are those of the authors and not necessarily those of the Institute, its officers, directors, or others associated with, or funding, its work.

Library of Congress Cataloging-in-Publication Data

America's purpose : new visions of U.S. foreign policy / edited by
   Owen Harries.
       p.   cm.
   Includes index.
   ISBN 1-55815-131-1 (cloth) $19.95
   1. United States—Foreign relations—1989–   I. Harries, Owen.
E881.A45   1991   327.73—dc20   90-23276

CONTENTS

Contents

FOREWORD

The Persian Gulf War makes clear the heavy responsibilities that America, the world's only true superpower, bears. How should we exercise our power? In *America's Purpose,* sixteen strategic thinkers offer a new vision of American might. Together these chapters form a handbook of alternative U.S. foreign policies for the 1990s.

These chapters were first published in the *National Interest,* a journal edited by Owen Harries that in but five years of existence has become essential to an understanding of modern politics among nations. *America's Purpose* explores the timeless questions of foreign policy: Internationalism or isolationism? Realism or moralism? What is the national interest? How Americans choose to answer these questions will shape international relations—and indeed, America—for years to come.

—Robert B. Hawkins, Jr., President
Institute for Contemporary Studies

AMERICA'S
PURPOSE

INTRODUCTION

OWEN HARRIES

Since the fall of 1989 it has been evident to all but the incorrigibly pessimistic that the Cold War is over and that the United States has won.

This outcome, long sought, is to be devoutly welcomed. But at the same time it must be acknowledged that winning the Cold War involves a certain disorientation, even a sense of deprivation. By and large, we knew where we were and what we were about during the Cold War. For one thing, it had been around a long time—for the entire adult life of anyone not yet sixty-five—and was thoroughly familiar. For another, it represented a remarkably simple and graspable state of affairs, with a designated enemy, long-standing allies, and fixed strategies. Third, and in some ways most important, the Cold War came complete with a built-in sense of a higher purpose that was morally and ideologically fulfilling. This was not just a selfish struggle for gain between two groups of states; great issues of freedom and justice were involved.

Now, with little time to prepare ourselves, we have been deprived of all that. Not only are we in a country without maps, but we have no clear marching orders or agreed destination. Nor is it clear which of the now deeply ingrained habits of thought and behavior acquired during the long years of the Cold War are going to be a help and which a hindrance in our new circumstances.

All this matters rather more to Americans than to others. In anything except a shooting war, the experience of the United States as a fully engaged great power is restricted almost entirely to the peculiar bipolar and high-octane conditions of the Cold War. Its image of itself as a "superpower"—an image to which it may be more attached than it realizes—was shaped by those atypical circumstances, and the country has little other experience to fall back on.

As well as this, many good judges (though not all) believe that an American foreign policy can be effective and sustainable only if it embodies and reflects some large moral or ideological purpose. To the extent that this is true, the Cold War's zero-sum, Manichaean struggle between democratic virtue and totalitarian evil was ideally suited to the American temperament—and the ending of that struggle raises the question of what now is to provide that larger sense of purpose, if indeed it is deemed to be still necessary.

It is against this background that the *National Interest* asked sixteen eminent commentators to reflect on what the central purpose of American foreign policy should be in the post–Cold War world. Most, though again, not all, of the contributors are conservatives or neoconservatives, but they are anything but agreed in their views. Some see the Cold War as having been a special, aberrant case in the American experience and maintain that now that it is over it is time for America to "come home" and return to an earlier pattern of behavior based on a much more restricted view of the country's interests and commitments. At the other end of the spectrum it is argued that, having just won a great victory and become the world's only genuine super-power, the United States should exploit its primacy, accept its historic mission, and "wage democracy" throughout the world. Some stress prudence, others boldness; some assert America's continuing "exceptionalism," some its new-found normality; some look to America's origins for guid-ance, some to the imperatives imposed by new economic and technological facts.

As well as casting light on the choices confronting America at the end of the twentieth century, then, this vol-ume also illuminates the differences among conservatives as the cement of anticommunism dissolves away. These differences—expressed here without inhibition, and often in sharp, colorful, and provocative language—are taken by some to be evidence of disintegration and weakness. I be-lieve they are better interpreted as a sign of intellectual and political vitality, diversity, and confidence, currently un-matched elsewhere on the American political spectrum.

In fairness to the authors it should be pointed out that all wrote before Iraq invaded Kuwait and precipitated the war in the Persian Gulf. Texts have not been amended to take account of that development; instead they remain as a record of how things appeared to a distinguished group of commentators in that brief interval of time between the end of the Cold War and the beginning of the first post–Cold War crisis.

I

UNIVERSAL DOMINION

CHARLES KRAUTHAMMER

All discussions of American purpose in the post–Cold War world must begin with the proviso that first we get to post. The primary task of American diplomacy—its task for, say, the next decade—is to win the Cold War. Ending the Cold War on Western terms, now for the first time within reach, means the Findlandization of Stalin's inner empire (Eastern Europe), the decolonization of Brezhnev's outer empire (the Third World satrapies in Africa, Asia, and Central America), and the continued liberalization of the center (the politics and economy) of the Soviet Union itself.

Since my purpose here is to discuss what comes after, I will not dwell on how victory is to be pursued, except to say that since it was containment and competition, military and economic, that ultimately prevailed in the Cold War, it would be historic folly to relax our grip just when success is in sight. In some ways, we are in a position analogous to that of the allies after the Normandy invasion. Victory is inevitable, so long as we don't stop.

Most interesting now, as then, is the problem of two-tiered thinking: how to win the current war while at the same time preparing for the postwar world. America did not do very good two-tiered thinking on the road to Berlin. The subsequent Cold War was, in part, a consequence of that poor thinking. It is particularly important, therefore, on the road to Moscow, as it were, to think about what comes after.

Assuming the Cold War is carried through to a successful conclusion, what then? Before asking what do we do, we must ask what the world will look like. It seems fairly clear that what will emerge is a multipolar system that retains some elements of bipolarity. The United States (certainly) and the USSR (probably) will remain qualitatively superior powers as nuclear-armed, continental states with the ability to project power to almost any place on earth. China, Japan, and some kind of confederated Western Europe will constitute the other major players (though a reunified Germany could well emerge in the next century as an independent actor). With ideology bleached from the system, it will resemble the balance-of-power world of the late nineteenth century (or, as Owen Harries insists, the eighteenth).

What purpose have we in such a world? One can already see the lines of argument developing. Indeed, the debate has broken out with some fury, perhaps a decade before the fact, in conservative ranks, where the ancient pull of classical isolationism remains strong and is just beginning to declare itself publicly. What purpose have we in a world without communism? None, beyond the narrowest defense of our national security, say the paleoconservatives.

In his notorious Heritage Foundation speech of October 1988, Russell Kirk pointed the way, denouncing neoconservative "cultural and economic imperialists" bent on "pursuing a fanciful democratic globalism rather than the national interest of the United States." With characteristic candor, Patrick J. Buchanan followed with a newspaper column that said bluntly: "When this Cold War is over, America should come home."

At the other pole are indeed some neoconservative thinkers who would urge upon the United States a return to an updated Wilsonianism: With the decline of communism, the advancement of democracy should become the touchstone of a new ideological American foreign policy. Whether it is National Endowment for Democracy money for Solidarity printing presses or American troops to redeem a stolen Panamanian election, American purpose is the democratic crusade. What purpose have we in a world without communism? Same as before, say the neoconservatives, only more so. Communism may be dead, but the work of democracy is never done.

There will soon be a similar split among liberals, though they are not yet aware of it. Some will continue the post-Vietnam McGovern tradition of frank "Come Home America" isolationism. Ultimately they will find themselves on the same side of the fence as the conservative isolationists, much as Norman Thomas and Robert Taft were de facto foreign policy allies in the 1930s.

The other strain of post-Vietnam liberalism is internationalist. Its ideal is the worldwide human rights campaign as envisioned by Jimmy Carter. These liberal internationalists, like the neoconservatives, think America has a mission beyond narrowly defined national interest. Neoconservatives call that mission democracy. Liberals call it human rights. There will soon be less to this argument than meets the eye. Under Carter, liberals tried to promote human rights in the abstract, as an end in itself. Conservatives argued that democracy is the indispensable structural condition for the success of human rights. There is, however, no longer a great gulf between the two camps on the issue because conservatives have won the argument. Liberals, particularly since the experience of Poland and Hungary, are beginning to agree that true progress on human rights requires a democratic structure and that unless institutions are liberalized, human rights victories—the release of some political prisoners, the relaxation of certain oppressive measures—are likely to be ephemeral.

Moreover, another factor that heretofore aggravated the fight between conservative and liberal internationalists—the preoccupation of the former with communist tyrannies and the latter with the "authoritarian" type—will wane. In a post–Cold War world, where communism is a spent force, there will be little to divide these adversaries. Left and Right internationalists will find common cause as they did in the early postwar years.

The result will be startling. The Left–Right debate of today will gradually transform itself into the isolationist–internationalist debate of yesterday. The alliances will be a crazy quilt. In the end, however, neither the isolationist nor the internationalist position will satisfy.

I have been closely associated with the pro-democracy internationalist school during the 1980s. I have some doubts, however, whether in the radically changed post-communist world that we are postulating, the democratic crusade should be the central plank of an American foreign policy.

Why should it make a difference for the promotion of democracy whether we are in a Cold War or post–Cold War world? It makes a great difference. During the Cold War the United States has been involved in a struggle to preserve a *structure* of freedom in the world. The necessary condition for what John F. Kennedy called the "success of liberty" was the defeat of those great forces—fascism and communism—which threatened the very idea of freedom and had the power and will to execute the threat. By winning these victories, the United States has, literally, made the world safe for democracy.

For reasons of both American interests and American values, the responsibility to make democracy possible was a historical absolute. The responsibility to enact the next stage—to make democracy actual in every corner of the globe—is less controlling.

A great power undertakes great battles because no one else can. But with the great battle won, the question of whether to engage in the mop-up work is a very different one. A communist Nicaragua in isolation is far different from a communist Nicaragua as an outpost of the Soviet empire or as an outpost of communism as an armed creed. Assuming that the center of the empire, the metropolis, either changes or withers (which is how Gorbachev frames the choices now facing the Soviet Union), then the strategic meaning of the outer empire is radically altered—it becomes far less of a threat to American security narrowly defined and even less of a threat to the cause of freedom broadly defined.

Connection makes all the difference. If the connection is severed—if the Cold War is won—then the islands of tyranny in the world, isolated and unsupported by a massive imperial center, become not only less threatening, but more likely to wither, in isolation, from their own contradictions.

We should do what we can to encourage that withering. But, unlike containment, that process of encouragement does not rise to the rank of defining purpose of American foreign policy.

The isolationist position, on the other hand, is more easily dismissed. Today, as in the 1930s or 1950s, there is no safety in isolationism. True, American disengagement in a post–Cold War world would not have the immediate consequences that it would have had, say, in Stalin's time. But what the isolationist Left and Right fail to understand—they remember 1939 but forget 1914—is how fragile is the structure of peace even in the absence of ideological conflict. They ignore the indispensable role that the deployment of American power plays in the maintenance of global stability. There is nothing that would more destabilize Asia, for example, than the withdrawal of American troops from Japan. No country from South Korea to China to Thailand to Australia—not even Vietnam—fears the deployment of American troops. What they do fear is American withdrawal. Not that they expect immediate Japanese rearmament. But in absence of Pax Americana there would be enough nervousness about ultimate Japanese intentions and capabilities to spark a local arms race and create instability and tension of a kind that has not been seen in Asia for decades.

Isolationism and Wilsonian internationalism are not, however, the only alternatives open to the United States in a post–Cold War world. One alternative is classical realpolitik: to act as Britain did a century ago as the great balancer of power. America, an island continent and dominant naval power, is geographically suited and militarily equipped for the role. Unfortunately, it is entirely unfit psychologically. There is no stomach and very little tolerance in the United States for a foreign policy of realpolitik. The strain of

American moralism—whether it energizes an expansive internationalism or a self-righteous isolationism—is simply too powerful. (Anyone who doubts that should think only of the reaction when our premier realpolitician, Henry Kissinger, wrote of Tiananmen Square in terms too mildly critical of Deng.)

What then? I would propose yet another alternative, an entirely blue-sky idea: After having doubly defeated totalitarianism, America's purpose should be to steer the world away from its coming multipolar future toward a qualitatively new outcome—a unipolar world whose center is a confederated West.

In a sense, I am proposing the politics of the fiber optic cable. As the industrialized democracies become increasingly economically, culturally, and technologically linked, they should begin to think about laying the foundations for increasingly binding political connections. This would require the conscious depreciation not only of American sovereignty, but of the notion of sovereignty in general. Yet this is not as outrageous an idea as it sounds. In Europe today some of the greatest world powers of the last half millennium—Britain, France, Germany, Italy, Holland, Spain, and Portugal—are involved in what Robert Hormats correctly calls the single greatest voluntary transfer of sovereignty in world history.

Europe '92 would be the model for the larger integration of the new Europe with North America and democratic Asia. Nothing as dramatic as Europe '92 could be expected from noncontiguous states so divided by race and culture and language. Nevertheless, we can already see the embryonic mechanisms of the new super-sovereignty, mechanisms such as the G-7 and the G-5, which are beginning to act as a finance committee for the West.

How would this arrangement bring about unipolarity in the international system? Such a confederation could have no rival. Around it would radiate in concentric circles, first, the Second World, the decommunizing states, dependent on the West for technology and finance. As they liberalize economically and politically, they would become individually eligible for status as associate members of the unipolar center. The outer ring, even more dependent on the center, would consist of the developing states. Its graduates too (say, Korea, Brazil, Israel) might also eventually attach themselves to the center.

The goal, one might say, is the world as described by Francis Fukuyama in his essay "The End of History?"* Fukuyama's provocation was to assume that the end—what he calls the common marketization of the world—is either here or inevitably dawning. It is neither. The West has to make it happen, and for that, the United States has to wish it. It has to wish and work for a super-sovereign West economically, culturally, and politically hegemonic in the world.

How is this vision different from the naive nonsense of earlier one-world visions? The old universalism (circa 1945) of the United Nations variety was based on the fallacy that structure begets community: that once we established the parliament of man, a world community would begin to emerge from it. The new universalism is based on the contrary notion that community begets structure: that if one begins with community, the smaller community of Western democratic nations, out of it will emerge the universal structure to which others can attach themselves over time.

The other great fallacy of the old universalism was the belief that one could have a universal community with

* *The National Interest,* no. 16 (Summer 1989).

common purpose in the presence of fundamental ideological conflict. Only in a world where the totalitarian challenge has been abolished, where the contention of nations has replaced the clash of armed doctrines, is universal community even conceivable.

In its spirit and ultimate goal, this idea of a super-sovereign West is not far from that of the pro-democracy crusade. But its approach is radically different. It focuses on the center, not the periphery. It is based on the assumption that unification of the industrial West is the major goal of the democratic crusade, rather than the conversion, one by one, of the Third World states. It is based on the further assumption that the centripetal forces generated by continued Western success at the center will, as in the 1980s, lead inexorably to the spread of democracy to the Second and Third World. And that, therefore, out there is not the place to start as America searches for its new role in the world.

I have no idea whether this goal is achievable. I tend to think not, although perhaps it is no more unlikely than the unification of the French duchies might have seemed in the fifteenth century, or of the Italian city-states in the early nineteenth, or of Western Europe in 1939. Moreover, it is perhaps as unlikely that Americans are psychologically prepared to subsume their sovereignty in some kind of great Western confederation as they are to adopt nineteenth-century realpolitik. But we are dealing here with goals, not reality. If the new age dawns and some new national purpose is to be offered and sold the American people, I suggest that we go all the way and stop at nothing short of universal dominion.

2

IF THIS LONG WAR IS OVER . . .

NATHAN TARCOV

If the Soviet Union were to disintegrate or to turn inward and devote its energy and resources overwhelmingly to internal reform; *if* it were to radically reduce and alter its nuclear forces so as not to threaten the United States; *if* it were to reduce, withdraw, or drastically alter its conventional forces so as not to threaten our allies; *if* it were to terminate its support for client states whose armed forces threaten our friends; *if* it were to abandon its efforts and its support for the efforts of its clients to destabilize governments friendly to us; *if* it were to allow full independence to all the nations it has occupied; *if* it were to liberalize and democratize its own polity so as to allow public debate over its foreign and defense policy; *if* it were to cease anti-Western propaganda and disinformation both among its own people and abroad; in short, if the Soviet Union were no longer to pose a significant threat to the United States and its friends and allies, then meeting that

that threat could no longer be considered the central purpose of American foreign policy. What then would that purpose be?

It is helpful to approach this question by posing the following radical alternative: Would the United States try to claim victory in a competition the Soviet Union had forfeited or would it regard the competition as cancelled? Would the United States attempt to exercise a then practically uncontested world leadership or would it too turn inward and at best devote its energy and resources overwhelmingly to internal reform? Answering this question seems to depend less on whether one considers the Cold War an ideological as well as a geopolitical contest than on whether one understands the United States to have had essentially positive or essentially negative aims in the contest. American ideological aims in the Cold War have been susceptible of either positive (spreading democracy) or negative (containing communism or preventing aggression) conceptions. American geopolitical concern could similarly be conceived as an effort either to tilt the balance of power as far as possible in our favor or merely to maintain an already favorable balance against Soviet attempts to tilt it in their favor. One's expectations for American policy in the event of Soviet collapse, withdrawal, or conversion seem to depend, in other words, on whether one understands the United States to have been a status quo power with merely defensive aims as opposed to the Soviet Union understood as a revolutionary power with offensive aims.

The view of American aims in the Cold War as negative or defensive is plausible, since the initial underlying balance of power, measured in resources for potential military strength rather than current troop levels, was favorable to the United States. The United States, with its

Western European allies and their colonial empires, occupying western Germany and almost all of Japan, far exceeded in this respect the Soviet Union and the territories it managed to occupy at the end of World War II. Whereas the Soviet Union had to change the underlying balance to enjoy a securely favorable correlation of forces, the United States had only to preserve that balance or at most develop its potential. Nevertheless, Soviet open intention and apparent capability to alter that initial balance would have made it imperative even for an originally defensive United States to attempt to alter the situation further in its favor.

American Cold War aims appeared negative or defensive also because of our explicit emphasis on containment, on preventing or thwarting acts of aggression or subversion, and our public aversion to committing such acts ourselves. The Soviet Union was much more comfortable with openly calling for and assisting changes of regime in other countries.

The United States, however, remains explicitly founded on universal principles of human equality, individual rights, government by consent, and the right of peoples to alter or abolish their governments when destructive of these ends. This founding has always made the United States a revolutionary power with positive, potentially global, aims, albeit ones that limit the means of their own actualization by dictating respect for the consent of other peoples. American statesmen from the start have urged the American people to consider the effects of their conduct and example on the fate of the whole human race (*Federalist* 1 and 14); they have sought to recommend our form of government to the esteem and adoption of mankind (*Federalist* 10); and they have hoped to vindicate the honor of the human race by teaching moderation to powers that extend their dominion by force and fraud (*Federalist* 11).

The myth of early American "isolationism" obscures the unlimited or revolutionary aims that were pursued by limited and prudent means and on the basis of meager and precarious resources. Universal principles were understood by early American statesmen to require prudence for their application. The need for circumstantial judgments of costs, dangers, and opportunities, for sober attention to the facts of power and geography, did not detract, however, from their sense of the universality of the principles animating American foreign and domestic policy. Despite our growing distance from the revolutionary past, our lengthening experience with post-revolutionary dictatorship, and our increasing stakes in the stability of the status quo, many Americans have retained a propensity to welcome and support revolutions, from those against the French *ancien régime* and the Spanish–American empire even to those against Batista, the Shah, and Somoza.

The doctrines of the Cold War therefore moved with an historic logic from the Truman Doctrine's policy of supporting free peoples resisting attempted subjugation by armed minorities or by outside pressures to the Reagan Doctrine's policy of active support for resistance forces fighting communist tyranny. The tendency of negative or defensive formulations of American Cold War aims to become positive or offensive could already be seen in NSC 68, the most comprehensive statement of American objectives in our competition with the Soviet Union.* That document (prepared in February and March 1950 by an interdepartmental study group headed by Paul Nitze, then director of the Policy Planning

---

*NSC 68 in Thomas H. Etzold and John Lewis Gaddis, eds., *Containment: Documents on American Policy and Strategy, 1945– 1950* (New York: Columbia University Press, 1978), pp. 387–89.

Staff, and approved by Truman on September 30, 1950) insisted, in accordance with a liberalism emphasizing tolerance and diversity, that "in relations between nations, the prime reliance of the free society is on the strength and appeal of its idea, and it feels no compulsion sooner or later to bring all societies into conformity with it." This contrasted with NSC 68's account of the fundamental design of the Kremlin's oligarchy to subvert or destroy the machinery of government and structure of society in the countries of the non-Soviet world. It was this implacable purpose which was supposed to have placed the two great powers at opposite poles and to have given their polarization the quality of crisis. This contrast between offensive Soviet aims and nonoffensive American aims, however, was paradoxically derived from an opposite contrast: The idea of freedom—"the most contagious idea in history"—is "peculiarly and intolerably subversive of the idea of slavery" whereas "the converse is not true." For NSC 68, it was the intrinsically offensive or subversive character of the American idea of freedom that made that idea "a permanent and continuous threat" to the foundations of Soviet society and that lay at the root of Soviet expansion. Thus ultimately it seemed to be the subversive character of American freedom that indirectly compelled the United States, despite our supposedly lacking a felt need to bring other societies into conformity with us, to adopt as an official aim "to foster a fundamental change in the nature of the Soviet system," albeit in the first place by negatively frustrating the design of the Soviet Union. So intimately connected were negative and positive formulations of American objectives.

The Cold War was not the first time that the United States revealed a tendency to think of its existence, success, and power as a threat subversive of despotism elsewhere and to expect to be so perceived by both despots and their subjects.

In the era of the Holy Alliance, Americans also expected powerful despotic societies to regard us as a threat and therefore to become a threat to us by seeking to eliminate our dangerous example. It would almost be an insult if such societies did not so regard us and validate our self-understanding. With greater power and vulnerability than in earlier eras, the American superpower could aim to eliminate powerful despotisms before they could eliminate us.

If the Soviet Union should now or at some point in the near future be regarded "essentially as another great power like other great powers," as George Kennan recently recommended, it does not necessarily follow that the *United States* should be regarded essentially as another great power like other great powers.* It would no longer be one of two superpowers animated by antagonistic universal principles and its behavior would alter accordingly. Countering the Soviet threat would no longer be the central purpose of its foreign policy, but fulfilling the American promise could then become that central purpose.

Remaining faithful to the positive and global character of American objectives after the Cold War should not involve doctrinaire crusading or reckless disregard for the value of American resources, the costs and risks of particular policies, and the choices of other peoples. Even and perhaps especially an unprecedented opportunity for world leadership would require prudence for its safe and successful exercise. Still we should not, for example, regard the relative rise in power of our allies as cancelling the relative decline of our

---

*George F. Kennan, testimony before the Senate Committee on Foreign Relations, *The Future of U.S.–Soviet Relations: Overview,* April 4, 1989, as quoted by Daniel Patrick Moynihan, *The National Interest,* no. 16 (Summer 1989), p. 32.

antagonist. It implies only that we must often claim the fruits of victory by exercising leadership rather than through unilateral action, just as we often must do so through formal or informal agreement with a retreating antagonist. Precisely the universality of our inspiration should make it easy to share a victory that can be understood at least as much as that of the peoples of the Soviet empire as it is of all those who have followed our lead.

For the United States to become essentially another great power like other great powers, presumably focusing exclusively on its own economic and security interests, it would have to lose its dedication to its universal founding principles much as the Soviet Union seems to be doing with Marxism-Leninism. Such a conversion from universalism to particularism is not imminent, but neither is it inconceivable. Diverse segments of our intellectual and academic opinion makers seek to generate or at least would welcome such a transformation, whether for reasons of foreign or domestic policy or from theoretical perspectives that hold our claim to rational universalism to be only the most domineering irrational particularism.

The prospect of shedding our universalist claims and superpower responsibilities tempts us with a relaxing concentration on our domestic comforts and corruptions. But the Soviet example suggests troubling dimensions of that prospect. Losing the universalist convictions that held it together may bring the disintegration of such an entity into its particularist ethnic, religious, and linguistic fractions. In the American case, those fractions do not coincide with our federated governments and neither pose the secessionist dangers nor generate the countervailing centralism that mark the Union of Soviet Socialist Republics. The United States cannot easily become an ordinary, tribal country constituted by blood, language, and religion, but it can become a cacophony of contending tribes—blacks, Hispanics, and Christian fundamentalists among others. And on the level of international relations, while it is difficult to wax nostalgic over the order and stability brought to certain regions by the waning superpower role of the Soviet Union, it is easy to foresee anarchic dangers incident to any American retreat from leadership.

The fulfillment of the list of hypothetical conditions at the start of this essay may well postpone indefinitely the stark alternative posed here. Meanwhile, elements of competition with the Soviet Union are likely to accompany either alternative. Soviet military power is likely to constrain either American victory or American withdrawal, just as it constrained containment, with the imperative to avoid war between the superpowers. While doing our best to navigate a complicated and contradictory period of transition, it should nonetheless be helpful to contemplate the ultimate alternatives.

3

AMERICA FIRST—
AND SECOND, AND THIRD

PATRICK J. BUCHANAN

On the birthday of Thomas Jefferson, dead half a decade, the president of the United States raised his glass, and gave us, in a six-word toast, our national purpose: "The Union," Old Hickory said, "it must be preserved."

It was to "create a more perfect Union" that the great men came to Philadelphia; it was to permit the Republic to grow to its natural size that James K. Polk seized Texas and California; it was to preserve the Union—not end slavery—that Lincoln invaded and subjugated the Confederate states.

"A republic if you can keep it," Franklin told the lady in Philadelphia. Surely, preservation of the Republic, defense of its Constitution, living up to its ideals—that is our national purpose. "America does not go abroad in search of monsters to destroy," John Quincy Adams said. "She is the well-wisher of the freedom and independence of all. She is the champion and vindicator only of her own."

Yet when the question is posed, "What is America's national purpose?" answers vary as widely as those who take it. To Randall Robinson of TransAfrica, it is the overthrow of South Africa; to Jesse Jackson, it is to advance "justice" by restoring the wealth the white race has robbed from the colored peoples of the earth; to the American Israel Public Affairs Committee, it is to keep Israel secure and inviolate; to Ben Wattenberg, America's "mission" is a crusade to "wage democracy" around the world. Each substitutes an extranational ideal for the national interest; each sees our national purpose in another continent or country; each treats our Republic as a means to some larger end. "National purpose" has become a vessel, emptied of original content, into which ideologues of all shades and hues are invited to pour their own causes, their own visions.

In Charles Krauthammer's "vision" (Chapter 1), the "wish and work" of our nation should be to "integrate" with Europe and Japan inside a "super-sovereign" entity that is "economically, culturally, and politically hegemonic in the world." This "new universalism," he writes, "would require the conscious depreciation not only of American sovereignty but of the notion of sovereignty in general. This is not as outrageous as it sounds."

While Krauthammer's super-state may set off onanistic rejoicing inside the Trilateral Commission, it should set off alarm bells in more precincts than Belmont, Massachusetts. As national purpose, or national interest, like all of the above, it fails the fundamental test: Americans will not fight for it.

Long ago, Lord Macaulay wrote:

> And how can man die better
> Than facing fearful odds,
> For the ashes of his fathers,
> And the temples of his Gods.

A nation's purpose is discovered not by consulting ideologies, but by reviewing its history, by searching the hearts of its people. What is it for which Americans have always been willing to fight?

Let us go back to a time when the establishment wanted war, but the American people did not want to fight.

In the fall of 1941, Europe from the Pyrenees to Moscow, from the Arctic to North Africa, was ruled by Hitler's Third Reich. East of Moscow, Stalin's gulag extended across Asia to Manchuria, where it met the belligerent Empire of the Rising Sun whose domain ran to mid-Pacific. England was in her darkest hour. Yet, still, America wanted to stay out; we saw, in the world's bloody conflict, no cause why our soldiers should be sent overseas to spill a single drop of American blood. Pearl Harbor, not FDR, convinced America to go to war.

The isolationism of our fathers is today condemned, and Roosevelt is adjudged a great visionary because he sought early involvement in Britain's war with Hitler. But even the interventionists' arguments were, and are, couched in terms of American national interest. Perhaps we did not see it, we are told, but our freedom, our security, our homes, our way of life, our Republic, were at risk. Thus do even the acolytes of interventionism pay tribute to the true national interests of the United States, which are not to be found in some hegemonic and utopian world order.

When Adams spoke, he was echoing Washington's Farewell Address that warned his fickle countrymen against inveterate antipathies against particular nations and passionate attachments for others. The nation, which indulges toward another an habitual hatred, or an habitual fondness, is in some degree a slave. It is a slave to its animosities or to its affections, either of which is sufficient to lead it astray from its duty and its interest.

For a century after Washington's death, we resisted the siren's call of empire. Then Kipling's call to "Take up the white man's burden" fell upon the receptive ears of Bill McKinley, who came down from a sleepless night of consulting the Almighty to tell the press that God had told him to take the Philippines. We were launched.

Two decades later, 100,000 Americans lay dead in France in a European war begun, as Bismarck predicted it would begin, "because of some damn fool thing in the Balkans."

"To make the world safe for democracy," we joined an alliance of empires, British, French, and Russian, that held most of mankind in colonial captivity. Washington's warning proved prophetic. Doughboys fell in places like the Argonne and Belleau Wood, in no small measure to vindicate the Germanophobia and Anglophilia of a regnant Yankee elite. When the great "war to end war" had fertilized the seed bed that produced Mussolini, Hitler, and Stalin, Americans by 1941 had concluded a blunder had been made in ignoring the wise counsel of their Founding Father.

After V-E Day and V-J Day, all America wanted to "bring the boys home," and we did. Then they were sent back, back to Europe, back to Asia, because Americans were persuaded—by Joseph Stalin—that the Cold War must be waged, because Lenin's party had made the United States the "main enemy" in its war against the West. As the old saw goes, you can refuse almost any invitation, but when a man wants to fight, you have to oblige him.

If the Cold War is ending, what are the terms of honorable peace that will permit us to go home? Are they not withdrawal of the Red Army back within its own frontiers, liberation of Central Europe and the Baltic republics, reunification of Germany, and de-Leninization of Moscow—that is, overthrow of the imperialist party that has prosecuted the Seventy Years' War against the West?

Once Russia is rescued from Leninism, its distant colonies, Cuba and Nicaragua, must eventually fall, just as the outposts of Japan's Empire, cut off from the home islands, fell like ripe apples into the lap of General MacArthur. Withdrawal of the Red Army from Europe would remove from the hand of Gorbachev's successor the military instrument of Marxist restoration.

The compensating concession we should offer: total withdrawal of U.S. troops from Europe. If Moscow will get out, we will get out. Once the Red Army goes home, the reason for keeping a U.S. army in Europe vanishes. Forty years after the Marshall Plan, it is time Europe conscripted the soldiers for its own defense.

As the Austrian peace treaty demonstrates, troop withdrawals are the most enduring and easily verifiable form of arms control. If we negotiate the 600,000 troops of the Red Army out of Central Europe, they cannot return, short of launching a new European war.

There is another argument for disengagement. When the cheering stops, there is going to be a calling to account for the crimes of Tehran, Yalta, and Potsdam, where the Great Men acceded to Stalin's demand he be made cartographer of Europe. In the coming conflicts—over Poland's frontiers east and west, over Transylvania, Karelia, Moldavia, the breakup of Yugoslavia—our role is diplomatic and moral, not military.

In 1956, at the high-water mark of American power, the United States stood aside as Soviet tanks crushed the Hungarian revolution. With that decision, Eisenhower and Dulles told the world that, while we support freedom in

Central Europe, America will not go to war with Russia over it. The year of revolution, 1989, revealed the logical corollary: From Berlin to Bucharest to Beijing, as Lord Byron observed, "Who would be free, themselves must strike the first blow."

Would America be leaving our NATO allies in the lurch? Hardly. NATO Europe contains fourteen states, which, together, are more populous and three times as wealthy as a Soviet Union deep in an economic, social, and political crisis. Moreover, NATO would have a new buffer zone of free, neutral, anticommunist nations between the Soviet and German frontiers. Our job will have been done.

To conquer Germany, the Red Army would have to cross a free Poland of 500 miles and 40 million people, before reaching the frontier of a united Reich of 80 million, whose tradition is not wholly pacifist. In the first hours of invasion, Moscow would see her economic ties to the West severed, and a global coalition forming up against her, including Germany, France, Britain, China, Japan, and the United States. As the Red Army advanced, it would risk atomic attack. To what end? So the Kremlin can recapture what the Kremlin is giving up as an unwanted and unmanageable empire?

The day of the realpoliticians, with their Metternichian "new architectures," and balance-of-power stratagems, and hidden fear of a world where their op-ed articles and televised advice are about as relevant as white papers from Her Majesty's Colonial Office, is over.

Why seek a united Germany? Because it is consistent with our values, our promise to the German people, and our national interest. Moreover, the Germans desire it, and will attain it. "Conditions" set down by President Bush and Secretary Baker will prove as ineffectual as they are insulting. (If the Germans decide to unite, what, exactly, would we do to stop them: Occupy Munich until they yield to our demand that they stay in NATO?)*

A free, united Germany in the heart of Europe, inoculated against Marxism by forty-five years of the disease, would be a triumph of American policy, a pillar of Western capitalism, and the first line of defense against a resurgent Russian imperialism. For the United States to permit itself to be used by London, Paris, and Moscow to impede reunification is to reenact, seventy years later, the folly of Versailles. Deny Germans the unity they rightly seek, and we shall awake one morning to find the Russians have granted it.

But disengagement does not mean disarmament. Still the greatest trading nation on earth, the United States depends for its prosperity on freedom of the seas. The strength of the U.S. Navy should be nonnegotiable; and, when the president is invited to enter naval arms control negotiations, the answer should be no, even if it means Moscow walks out.

With the acquisition of ballistic missiles by China, Iran, Iraq, Syria, and Libya, with atomic weapons work being done in half a dozen countries of the Third World, the United States needs—nay, requires—a crash research and development program for missile defense, to protect our homeland, our warships, our bases. No arms control agreement is worth trading away the Strategic Defense Initiative.

An island-continent, America should use her economic and technological superiority to keep herself permanent mistress of the seas, first in air power, first in space.

*Since this essay was written, Germany has, of course, been reunited unconditionally. —ED.

Nor is the cost beyond our capacity. For it is not warships and weapons that consume half our defense budget; it is manpower and benefits. When defense cuts are made, they should come in army bases, no longer needed for home-land defense, and ground troops no longer needed on foreign soil.

As U.S. bases close down in Europe, we should inform Moscow we want all Soviet bases closed in the Caribbean and Central America, all Soviet troops out of the Western hemisphere. They have no business here. This is our hemi-sphere; and the Monroe Doctrine should be made again the cornerstone of U.S. foreign policy.

As the United States moves off the mainland of Europe, we should move our troops as well off the mainland of Asia. South Korea has twice the population and five times the economic might of North Korea. She can be sold the planes, guns, missiles, and ships to give her decisive superiority; then, U.S. troops should be taken out of the front line.

We are not going to fight another land war in Asia; no vital interest justifies it; our people will not permit it. Why, then, keep 30,000 ground troops on the demilitarized zone? If Kim Il Sung attacks, why should Americans be first to die? If we must intervene, we can do so with air and sea power, without thousands of army and marine dead. It is time we began uprooting the global network of "trip wires" planted on foreign soil to ensnare the United States in the wars of other nations, to back commitments made and treaties signed before this generation of American sol-diers was ever born.

The late Barbara Tuchman wrote of the Kaiser that he could not stand it if somewhere in the world a quarrel was going on and he was not a party to it. Blessed by Providence with pacific neighbors, north and south, and vast oceans, east and west, to protect us, why seek permanent entanglement in other people's quarrels?

The beginning of the end of the Cold War is surely time for that "agonizing reappraisal" of which Dulles only spoke. As Chesterton said, one ought not tear down a wall until you know why it was put up, but we must begin asking why some walls were built, and whether maintaining them any longer serves *our* interests.

As we ascend the staircase to the twenty-first century, America is uniquely situated to lead the world. Japan has a population older and not half as large as ours; her land and resources cannot match California's. Even united, the two Germanies have but a third of our population, a fifth of our GNP, and a land area smaller than Oregon and Washington. Neither Japan nor Germany is a nuclear power; neither has a navy or air force to rival ours; even their combined GNP is dwarfed by ours. While the Soviet Union has the size, resources, and population to challenge us as a world power, she is a prison house of nations whose ethnic hatreds and unworkable system mean a decade of turmoil. Who is left? The corrupt, bankrupt China of Deng Xiaoping? It will not survive the decade. Nakasone was right: The twentieth century was the American century. The twenty-first century will also be the American century.

But America can lead the world into the twenty-first century only if she is not saddled down by all the baggage piled up in the twentieth.

For fifty years, the United States has been drained of wealth and power by wars, cold and hot. Much of that expenditure of blood and treasure was a necessary investment. Much was not.

We cannot forever defend wealthy nations that refuse to defend themselves; we cannot permit endless transfusions of the life blood of American capitalism into the mendicant countries and economic corpses of socialism, without bleeding to death. Foreign aid is an idea whose time has passed. The communist and socialist world now owe the West a thousand billion dollars and more, exclusive of hundreds of billions we simply gave away. Our going-away gift to the globalist ideologues should be to tell the Third World we are not sending the gunboats to collect our debts, but nor are we sending more money. The children are on their own.

Americans are the most generous people in history. But our altruism has been exploited by the guilt-and-pity crowd. At home, a monstrous welfare state of tens of thousands of drones and millions of dependents consumes huge slices of the national income. Abroad, regiments of global bureaucrats siphon off billions for themselves, their institutions, their client regimes. With the Cold War ending, we should look, too, with a cold eye on the internationalist set, never at a loss for new ideas to divert U.S. wealth and power into crusades and causes having little or nothing to do with the true national interest of the United States.

High among these is the democratist temptation, the worship of democracy as a form of governance and the concomitant ambition to see all mankind embrace it, or explain why not. Like all idolatries, democratism substitutes a false god for the real, a love of process for a love of country.

When we call a country "democratic," we say nothing about whether its rulers are wise or good, or friendly or hostile; we only describe how they were chosen, a process that produced Olaf Palme, José López Portillo, Pierre Trudeau, Sam Nujoma, Kurt Waldheim, and the Papandreous, *père et fils*, as well as Ronald Reagan.

Raúl Alfonsín, elected president, led Argentina to ruin; while General Pinochet, who seized power in a coup, rescued Chile from Castroism and leaves her secure, prosperous, and on the road to freedom. Why, then, celebrate Alfonsín and subvert Pinochet?

As cultural traditions leave many countries unsuited to U.S.–style democracy, any globalist crusade to bring its blessings to the natives everywhere must end in frustration, and will surely be marked by hypocrisy. While the National Endowment for Democracy meddles in the affairs of South Africa, the State Department props up General Mobutu. Where is the consistency?

Democracies, too, place their own selfish interests first. India, the world's largest, supported Moscow's genocidal war of annexation in Afghanistan, while General Zia, an autocrat, died aiding the resistance. Who was the true friend of liberty?

In 1936, Franco rescued Spain from a corrupt "democracy"; in 1937, Hitler received a "democratic" mandate from the German people; in 1941, Britain declared war on Finland, a democracy, at the behest of Stalin; in 1942, we deprived our own fighting men of needed weapons to send them to the USSR, the most contemptuous enemy democracy has ever known.

How other people rule themselves is their own business. To call it a vital interest of the United States is to contradict history and common sense. And for the Republic to seek to dictate to 160 nations what kind of regime each should have is a formula for interminable meddling and endless conflict; it is a textbook example of that "messianic globaloney" against which Dean Acheson warned; it is, in scholar Clyde Wilson's phrase, a globalization of that degenerate form of Protestantism known as the Social Gospel.

"We must consider first and last," Walter Lippmann wrote in 1943, "the American national interest. If we do not, if we construct our foreign policy on some kind of abstract theory of rights and duties, we shall build castles in the air. We shall formulate policies which in fact the nation will not support with its blood, its sweat, and its tears." Exactly.

What do Tibetans, *mujahedeen,* UNITA rebels, and *contras* have in common? Not belief in a bicameral legislature, or in separation of church and state, but love of liberty and a hatred of communism. Is it not that spirit of patriotism that brought down the vassal regimes of Central Europe, that today threatens to tear apart the Soviet Empire?

"Enlightened nationalism" was Mr. Lippmann's idea of a foreign policy to protect America's true national interest. What we need is a new nationalism, a new patriotism, a new foreign policy that puts America first, and, not only first, but second and third as well.

— 4 —

FREEDOM REMAINS
THE TOUCHSTONE

CARL GERSHMAN

With the stunning collapse of communism in Central Europe, it is appropriate to reconsider the goals of American foreign policy in a post–Cold War world. It is true, of course, that the communist regime in the Soviet Union remains in place, that in military terms Moscow is still a superpower, and that it continues to give military assistance to Afghanistan, Cuba, Angola, and other Third World client states. Nonetheless, the Soviet Union is exhausted economically and ideologically, and is in the throes of a profound systemic crisis. The challenge ahead is not to defend against its expansion but to manage its decline.

In this altered world, the policy of containment is clearly outdated. It does not respond to the immediate challenge of consolidating democratic systems in the liberated countries of Central Europe and facilitating their eventual integration into an expanded European community. It is rapidly becoming obsolete in the Third World as well.

That said, however, it does not follow that the United States must define a new "central purpose" for its foreign policy. Containment itself was not the central purpose of U.S. policy but rather a response to a specific geopolitical situation in which the United States found itself challenged by a formidable military and ideological rival. The central purpose, as stated in the Truman Doctrine, was to "support free peoples" in defense of a "way of life" based upon "the will of the majority" and "distinguished by free institutions, representative government, free elections, guarantees of individual liberty, freedom of speech and religion, and freedom from political oppression." Support for this way of life against its totalitarian alternative was the purpose for which containment was designed. The attenuation of the totalitarian challenge does not invalidate this purpose, which was enunciated before the Cold War by Woodrow Wilson and Franklin D. Roosevelt. It only raises the question of whether a policy of support for free institutions and for adherence to democratic political norms around the world can and should be sustained in the absence of a grave threat that necessitates U.S. action.

In answering that question, it may be helpful to recall that the consensus supporting the containment policy broke down as a result of the debate over U.S. involvement in Vietnam and was not reestablished during the following two decades. At issue was the policy of the United States toward noncommunist authoritarian governments threatened by communist attack or subversion. In effect, one side in this debate favored withdrawing the containment shield from such governments if they did not take meaningful steps to improve their human rights performance.

The other side favored retaining the shield not only to resist communist expansion but also in the belief that authoritarian systems were less repressive and more open to democratic reform than the totalitarian alternative.

The debate sharpened in the 1970s when it appeared that the United States faced the bleak prospect of having to choose between these two options only. It came to a head in 1979 over the Nicaraguan revolution, but the bitter lesson that each side came away with from that experience— that authoritarianism is not a bulwark against communism, and that the overthrow of authoritarianism is not a guarantee of democracy—actually laid the foundation for a new policy fostering peaceful transitions to democracy. As the democratic wave of the 1980s in Latin America and elsewhere in the Third World gained momentum, and despite the bitter dispute over funding the armed resistance to the Sandinista government in Nicaragua, a new bipartisan consensus began to form around this pro-democracy policy. In March 1986, following the peaceful revolution in the Philippines, President Reagan enunciated the new consensus by committing the United States to the "democratic revolution" taking place in the world. The core of his message to Congress was that "The American people believe in human rights and oppose tyranny in whatever form, whether of the Left or the Right."

The collapse of communism has given this policy renewed support as Republicans and Democrats outdo each other in calls for assistance to the democratic revolution in Central Europe, and as the fear of another Vietnam—still a cautionary factor in any policy expressing global support for democracy—recedes. Nonetheless, strong reservations persist about the merits of such a policy. They are associated with no single political camp, but can be found among both conservatives and liberals, as well as among foreign policy "realists" who have always been skeptical of American universalism.

The reservations may be summarized as follows: Democratic globalism, or Wilsonian internationalism if you will, betrays an ethnocentric point of view that mistakenly assumes democracy is an appropriate system for everybody. It is not, and the desire to implant it where it does not exist reflects cultural arrogance, missionary zeal, and a dangerous tendency to impose abstract principles on political reality. Moreover, a policy of globalism implies unlimited commitments along the lines of President Kennedy's pledge to "pay any price" to support freedom. If commitments exceed power and resources, policy will become insolvent, as Walter Lippmann once wrote. On top of this, there is no compelling, tangible national interest that is served by such a policy. The United States should not go abroad, in the famous words of John Quincy Adams, "in search of monsters to destroy," but only in pursuit of clearly defined interests to protect.

The response to this line of argument begins with the democratic revolution which demonstrates that successful democratic systems, as well as the aspiration for democracy, now extend far beyond the industrial democracies of the West. The last months of 1989 alone saw not only communist dictatorships overthrown in Central Europe but the holding of transitional elections in Chile, Namibia, and Taiwan; the peaceful transfer of power following sharply contested elections in the two largest Third World democracies, India and Brazil; and the installation of a democratically elected government in Panama (by U.S. troops, to be sure, but with the overwhelming approval of the Panamanian people). These dramatic events were the culmination of a period of unprecedented democratic gains that began in the 1970s with the democratic transitions in Greece, Spain, and Portugal, then spread across most of Central and South America and to a large part of Asia before it reached Central Europe. While the democratic movement in China was brutally suppressed, it probably did more than any single event to signal to the world that the democratic idea is truly universal and that there are young people continents and cultures away from the historic centers of democratic life who are prepared to lay down their lives for freedom. The democratic movement in Burma (which was suppressed) demonstrated the same point.

No single factor accounts for this worldwide phenomenon. The technological and communications revolutions have made the attributes of modern democratic society accessible and discernible throughout the world, thereby introducing into non-Western societies expectations and aspirations for democracy not present before. Moreover, the decline of traditional forms of authority in modernizing societies, combined with the more recent collapse of Marxism, has left democratic consent as the only means of conferring legitimacy on governments. Developing countries are also discovering that democracy, while by no means a panacea, offers a way to limit and decentralize state power, to expose corruption, to reduce the potential for civil violence by integrating different economic and ethnic groups into the system, and to achieve economic growth. As the alternative to tyrannical force in the management of increasingly complex societies, democracy would have to be invented, as Peter L. Berger has written, if it did not already exist.

If democracy is developing indigenously within countries because it offers the best way to manage the affairs of society and to achieve national objectives, the issue for us to decide is whether we should assist and encourage this process, not whether we should seek to impose our system on others. We cannot force others to do what they are not prepared or willing to do for themselves; the American people would not support this approach in any event. But we can insist upon adherence to political norms and provide support and encouragement to those seeking to establish democratic systems. Such a policy is consistent with American values—pluralism as well as democracy—and it does not risk insolvency because it can be pursued with relatively limited resources.

In fact, the basic elements of such a policy are already in place, having been assembled in the course of more than a decade of attempts to find common ground between liberals and conservatives, and between the executive branch and Congress, on these questions. They include the integration of human rights issues into the fabric of U.S. policy through such mechanisms as the establishment of a Human Rights Bureau at the State Department; the annual preparation of "country reports" on human rights; the conditioning of economic and security assistance, trade benefits, and votes in international lending agencies on human rights performance; and the provision of funds under the Foreign Assistance Act for programs that encourage respect for human rights. They also include instructions to U.S. ambassadors to carry out this policy by maintaining close contacts with democratic groups and by encouraging wherever possible steps toward stable democratic transitions. (The results of this activist approach have already been evident in such countries as the Philippines, Chile, Paraguay, Poland, and Hungary.)

An additional element in this policy has been the establishment of the National Endowment for Democracy, which enlists the involvement of private U.S. organizations—

principally institutes associated with our two political parties, the AFL–CIO, and the Chamber of Commerce—in assisting the development of democratic political and social institutions abroad. Military force is also an element in the policy, though its use is circumscribed by criteria, set forth by Defense Secretary Caspar Weinberger in 1984 and now widely endorsed, that favor the commitment of U.S. forces only as a last resort and only with broad bipartisan backing. Significantly, the commitment of U.S. forces in Panama and the show of force in the Philippines during the coup attempt against the Aquino government were justified in terms of supporting democracy.

But does this policy serve a compelling, tangible national interest? Or is it, to borrow the phrase of one commentator, "a special kind of international social work?" The events of late 1989 offer the most eloquent answer to this question, for it was the democratic revolution in Central Europe, more than any military or diplomatic factors, that brought the postwar era to a close and redrew the political map of the world. Despite all the attention devoted to disarmament over the last decades by governments and demonstrators alike, it was the success of the democratic struggles in the communist world that made meaningful disarmament a real possibility.

Beyond these immediate issues, the United States has a clear interest in the establishment of democratic governments abroad. Such governments are more likely than dictatorships to enjoy political stability and to establish peaceful relations with their neighbors. In addition, while governments that share our values may not agree with us on every issue, they are likely to be our friends and to desire a close mutual relationship. Just as important, we would be able to sustain such a close and collaborative relationship with *them,* something we have difficulty doing (given the nature of our polity and the importance we attach to democratic values) with countries that are not democratic. Moreover, given our position as the world's first and leading democracy, we have a unique opportunity to exercise leadership in supporting the progress of democracy, arguably the foremost political issue of our time. Our prestige and morale would inevitably suffer if we were to relinquish this responsibility.

Is the objective of supporting democracy sufficient to serve as a "central purpose" for the United States in its relations with the world? The question should answer itself, for this already *is* our central purpose and has been ever since our nation was founded on the basis of universal democratic principles. The moments when we strayed from these principles—during the Vietnam malaise, for example, when many Americans ceased to believe in our national purpose—have not been happy times for America. More recently, our national self-confidence and sense of purpose have been restored. The fact that this restoration coincided with the world democratic revolution may have been purely coincidental. More likely, however, these developments were mutually reinforcing; the former giving renewed impetus to the idea of freedom in the world, and the latter reminding us that our heritage does, indeed, have a universal meaning. That is a useful thing to recall as we set our course at the beginning of a new era.

5

TO SPEAK TO OURSELVES

MICHAEL VLAHOS

As we rush to embrace the new world, we have little time to reflect on what we leave behind. We should, because we haven't left it yet. We are in a transition, a bridge time; we sense a new reality, but still live in the old. And when we talk—about change, the future, America's purpose—we speak in the old language. Its powerful codewords still rule our subconscious. Most of us have only known this reality, this paradigm. When we think of beginnings, trying to imagine a new creation, we describe it with the slogans of the late 1930s and 1940s, when this old world was being built. That reality grew out of the received truths and myths of world war, prelude and postlude: Munich, Hitler–Stalin, the Bomb, Berlin. When Charles Krauthammer and Patrick J. Buchanan speak, as they have in these pages, it is with the passions of another time. They replicate the great argument in the drama that made that world: and suddenly, it is internationalism versus isolationism all over again. But only the language, the imagery.

Fifty years ago, the terms of debate hinged on the needs of America against the survival of the civilized world. Abstention from the world balance of power was then our national norm. Surely, the world was in trouble; but in saving the world, what would be left of us? And could it even be saved?

Today, engagement is the norm. The world has, arguably, been saved. The Krauthammer–Buchanan exchange (Chapters 1 and 3), however, is not just the old debate reversed. It is not, after all, the existential question reprised: to engage or to abstain. The era we are now departing has changed that forever. How?

When the postwar paradigm found its liturgy in NSC 68, world engagement meant a protracted, Manichaean struggle, at the end of which a U.S. global culture would triumph. The Free World would become one world, with the U.S.-bequeathed United Nations as its government.

Well folks, it didn't quite turn out that way. The Manichaean part may indeed be over, but the world looks nothing like what the paradigm creators expected back in the 1940s. Democracy is catching, but not as Americanism. They are not our little eaglets. Our world government-to-be has been forever despoiled, and our allies now emerge—the European Community and Japan—as equal world powers. This frets us because, along the way, we developed a taste for superpower. This is the unnamed, latent thought in today's debate about national purpose: What began as a crusade is ending as the lament of godhead lost. "We are still a superpower!" comes the cry. But the inner theme is loss.

Krauthammer turns Wilsonianism into frank imperialism, and he is up-front: "universal dominion." There is no better restatement of the postwar vision of a U.S. global culture, except now one supposes it is to be forced on others, not embraced by them. Has he asked the EC and Japan if they want to abridge their new-found integrity as world players to suit yet another ploy for U.S. domination? Will the Third World applaud our plan to gradually use their dependency to suck them into subservience? Buchanan wrestles mostly with the loss of U.S. power, responding both that it doesn't matter and that it isn't happening. To reassure himself he quotes Nakasone's condescending scrap for U.S. face-saving: "The twenty-first century will also be the American century."

Why do they both spend so much time worrying about our place in the world? You see, it really doesn't matter what we want. The world is going its own way, no matter how earnest our entreaties to the contrary. And much more important, America is going its own way too. World change unlocks change here, long repressed by the needs of global mission. What we—the beltway insiders, the archons of the Washington clubs, the fatted scions of an old power establishment—really fear is the loss of our social ranking, of our special imperial trusteeship when empire is gone. Will we still be important? What will happen to the imperial city now?

Before we ponder our own fate, let's look at what is really happening in the world. In our rhetoric, global crusade always announced its own eventual disestablishment. Kennedy spelled out the vision when he called for a "world safe for diversity." We simply assumed that this would be one-dimensional diversity: native garb and music, American democratic values—this is the "multipolar" world for which we waited. To turn early Christian theology about the nature of God just a bit, we looked to "one world, many operators."

The new world reality, however, is one of many worlds; or more correctly, a pantheon of many realities. In spite of the power and the glory of U.S. culture, the decolonized went their own way. Europe and Japan stuck by us . . . had they any choice? They were strategic dependents helpless in the face of raw evil. Now the evil mask is torn away, and both the European Community and Japan are moving toward self-realization. They are already our rough equal as economies; the recognition that they are full-fledged world powers is not far away. We remain warrior chieftain only through the transition.

After the transition, we may imagine a power balance built around three world powers—North America (USCAN), the EC, and Japan. These centers will drive the world economy, and will retain some measure of collegiality. They will also be engaged in ferocious competition—in which economic scrimmage over advantage in trade and technology will be the new game on the playing field of national security. It should be a time of great global economic growth; but however much we keep to fraternal handshakes, this competition will be the greatest challenge to the American way of life in the early twenty-first century. Europe and Japan will no longer be allies save in name.

Three great powers (a tier down from world powers) will cluster in Asia: Russia, China, and India. They will have roughly equivalent GNPs, science and technology, and military power. Russia may be more advanced but less martially inclined if it sheds restive republics; if it clings to empire, its army will be bigger, but its economy weaker. Indian growth will be steady; China should surge if it gets a popular new dynasty.

Other culture areas will remain diffuse, with some regional powers dominating and others competing: South

Africa will dominate Niger-Kordofanian Africa and Indonesia the Austronesian, for example, while the Arab-Islamic world will find no leader among sullen rivals.

The United States and Canada will come closer than ever through free trade union, and eventually pull in Mexico. USCAN will have no rival in its world, and will be free to move flexibly and forcefully in others. After the transition, we should be disentangled from our overseas "trip wires" (as Patrick J. Buchanan suggests in Chapter 3). So unencumbered, our strategic freedom of action will grow.

But this is all surface image. What are we doing? What are we all about? The answer to America's national purpose is to be found right here at home. Our approach to the world has always reflected our domestic agenda. This was just as true for the postwar era as any other. As we debate the course of world change, we forget that our old global mission mirrored a domestic paradigm, created by Franklin D. Roosevelt and sustained by a coherent party system and political establishment. It was a political model for America built on the bedrock premise of big government, or better yet, a crusading state that would lead America and the world to the Promised Land.

This vision's time is past. Its political establishment has lost the pulse of its own people. (Need we belabor the Democrats in their agony?) And the vision's promise itself gave out more than a decade ago. Failure in Vietnam was, after all, only the foreign reflection of a gathering failure of big government's domestic mobilization, its Great Society.

Americans today feel that this nation has lost its way. We see a welter of single issues burning in the political ether—from abortion to racism and its cures, to drugs, education, and the environment. With the savings and loan crisis, we talk about a failure of government, and now two-thirds of Americans want the length of congressional service limited. With abortion, we rage over moral decay versus even greater encroachment of government on individual liberty. With drugs, we are like helpless penitents scourging ourselves, in the face of a social plague that our great system cannot cure. With education, we are perplexed by a vast federal octopus actually abetting a decline in knowledge and skills among our youth. With the environment, many see the American Garden itself despoiled. Different vantages, same judgment: America corrupted. But these are only the fragments of visions of America yet to be patterned. They are like the tiny pieces of a mosaic, each expressing an intense part of the whole, linked by a pattern seen only from a distance. We do not yet have the distance.

When it comes to foreign policy, many Americans also feel that our own needs have been postponed by the claims of the great struggle, that we have sacrificed so long for others only to find ourselves weakened and astray. This is the unspoken content of the codeword "peace dividend," of cartoons showing Germany and Japan as the real postwar victors, of so many lamentations about national decline. Our foreign policy musings today are shot through with domestic melancholy.

In fact, it is almost irrelevant to talk about America's purpose when it is right here in front of us. The American idea is today at risk, and continuing an empty world crusade could kill it. Who are we? What do we stand for? What kind of society are we building? Renewing ourselves must come before any foreign relations: it must be our first priority. And world change that (for awhile) banishes old threats not only allows, but encourages, America to remake itself.

This brings us full circle to the foreign policy debate inside the beltway about America's purpose. The debaters are out of touch with the people they serve. The observer might even infer that we have come merely to serve ourselves. Accreting over half a century, Washington has become something both aberrant and unexampled in American eyes: an imperial metropole. The purpose for which it was established—internal as well as imperial state mobilization—no longer lives. But the great city does, resented as it is by the rest of the United States. This city and its establishment live to defend a fading reality; thus its inner debate cannot really address America's future course.

This truth must not be lost: What we do in the world for the good must come from a collective vision, strong and new within us. In the fifty years since our last Big Change (as Max Lerner calls it), the elite has become comfortable in, and dependent upon, our perpetual starring role: "United States, Superpower." The role became the end in itself, and for many it still is.

"Superpower" doesn't matter. The greatness of the American idea does. The urgent task ahead is one of remaking, reinterpreting. Choosing an American agenda for a new century outweighs all foreign claims. We simply cannot speak to the world until we can speak to ourselves.

What does this suggest for our actual approach to the world? First we must ditch the old debate of the 1930s and 1940s. The point now is not isolationism versus internationalism: We are strong today, not beaten down and afraid as we were in 1935. We could hardly be isolationists now if we tried. But no matter how hard we push, we cannot bring to life the universal spell of an American global culture. An opposite force is sweeping the world: Cultures repressed by Free World universalism (especially in Europe and Japan) are finding themselves again.

And they will be at best associates, not friends. The basis for trust will not pass the bar of the end of our postwar reality. We may have no enemies, but we will have no real allies either. Yes, they have imbibed a "democratic spirit" that we have spread. But once it is *their democracy*, it ceases to look to us for inspiration, and its political forms become more referent to native traditions. Arguably, as culture areas go their own way, so increasingly will their politics.

The practical foreign policy debate we should be having is how to deal with a time of parallel realities. The old paradigm is fading but it's not yet dead. Paradoxically, its claim on our passions is all the more wrenching (a death grip?) in its ending time. The new world reality still awaits the event to call it forth.

During the transition, we must try to imagine the next frame of reference while our day-to-day, operational energies are devoted to the task of gradually deconstructing the postwar world. This is the key to understanding the transition we are now in and the new world to come. The issues that seize us today are ones involving merely the managing of transition. They are not preparing us for what's ahead.

The transition period will demand the utmost of us: vigilance, forbearance, strength. We must see to the dismantling of Soviet (and then American) power in Europe, and stand guard as the Soviet slide works its way of imperial decline. When this transition ends, the new geopolitics can become American strategic opportunity. In it,

- What kind of challenges and threats do we face?

- How do we define national interest and responsibility?

- What military capabilities will be needed to defend us?

Threats: The security challenges we will face after the transition (post-2000) will be more moderate, if still significant. A national competition over technology will begin to describe a new balance of power with our former allies (the EC and Japan). Great powers and regional powers will fret and jostle. Economic bargaining will drive power diplomacy. Now there is no denying that the spirit of the age has turned against war; as in other true postwar times, we can expect war as a legitimate political tool to be in hiding for at least a decade. That peacetime bloom will darken, however, and the world of the next century will again find uses for military force, and in places, like space, where there are no earthly rules and precedents.

National Interest: Responsibility should be to ourselves first, and then to the promotion of a kind of global collegiality. We may wish to intrude ourselves at will (by sea, air, and space) in local potboilers, but we will intervene on the ground very selectively. U.S. interests will remain global, and we should stay interested in all that affects the global balance. But we will have the flexibility and relative strategic distance to choose when and how to get involved, if at all. In a pluralistic world where there are many powers, in which we may have no sworn enemies but also few real friends, a strategy of selective engagement gives the United States (or USCAN) the most leverage and the best chance to achieve our broader national goals through mediation rather than intervention.

Military Needs: We must keep the high ground. We will need non-nuclear, high-technology, low-manpower forces that we can bring to bear to support a strategy of global selective engagement. Our current advantage over all others in space and naval systems must be the focus of future American national security. Dominance in space and in the oceans will also support us in international technology competition; it will in effect be our insurance against the worst consequences of "multipolarity."

Let's face it: We cannot control world change to suit us; we cannot keep as our own the old world we've grown to like. The new world gives us room, however. The United States will not mature to be just another standard, historical cookie-cutter power on the scene. We will draw strength from the energies released in our renewal and continue to offer ourselves to the world. We can still, if we seize its primacy as our new mission, do best by looking again at ourselves, and the idea that made us.

6

DEFINING OUR
NATIONAL INTEREST

IRVING KRISTOL

It is very difficult for a great power—a world power—to articulate a foreign policy in the absence of an enemy worthy of the name. It is, after all, one's enemies that help define one's "national interest," in whatever form that definition might take. Without such enemies, one flounders amidst a plenitude of rather trivial, or at least marginal, options. That, it seems to me, is the condition of the United States today, as we enter the post–Cold War era.

I know that there are more than a few conservatives who bridle at the proposition that the Cold War is over. They point, for instance, to the fact—and it is a fact—that the Soviet Union's military capabilities are not at all diminished, and in some respects have actually increased under *glasnost*. They then go on to make the seemingly reasonable claim that it is by such a visible capability that we should judge Soviet foreign policy, not by inferences as to its intentions—inferences based either on rhetoric or on internal political developments of which we have only an imperfect understanding.

This sounds sensible enough, but it is nevertheless an error. Intention will always trump military capability in an analysis of a nation's foreign policy. After all, very few of the world's nations ever evaluated American foreign policy in terms of our impressive military capabilities. Only the Soviet Union and the other communist regimes, in the pre-Gorbachev era, ever thought along such lines, and the Soviet Union at least (and probably Communist China as well) now realizes that it was a mistake. Anyone who has a basic understanding of American society and American politics understands full well that this society and this politics put strict limits on the exercise of our military power. No one—except again, Soviet generals and politicians—ever believed for a moment that the United States was capable of launching a surprise nuclear attack against the Soviet Union—or against anyone else, for that matter. There were, for several decades now, many maleficent interpretations of American foreign policy floating around the world—usually having to do with something called "capitalism" or "economic imperialism" or "cultural imperialism." But none of these interpretations—again, always exempting communist regimes—derived from a fear of an abrupt onslaught by our military capabilities. The occasional rare exception, such as Libya, involved nations that had taken actions so blatantly hostile to the United States as practically to invite military retribution.

It is therefore interesting to note that it is only our military analysts of Soviet affairs who still focus on capabilities, whereas our political analysts, focusing on overall developments within the Soviet system, all concur that the

Cold War is indeed over. They agree that the Soviet Union today is simply impotent, lacking in the political energy, to sustain an intention of aggressive expansion. Moreover, it no longer even desires to. The classical and long-dominant Soviet intention, which properly alarmed much of the world, has withered away.

The best analysis of the condition of Soviet intentions today is to be found in a brilliant article by Stephen Sestanovich, "Inventing the Soviet National Interest."* In it Professor Sestanovich demonstrates conclusively that the Communist leadership and policy elites of the USSR, having abandoned (sometimes explicitly, sometimes implicitly) the Marxist-Leninist mode of thought, are struggling to rethink foreign policy from the ground up. "Where," they are openly wondering, "is the Russian national interest?" They are questioning the expensive investments of this near-bankrupt nation in such places as Cuba, Ethiopia, Vietnam, and elsewhere. "Of what use are these impoverished regimes to us?" they ask, and having forsaken the dream (now a nightmare) of World Communism, they are inclined to discover no use whatsoever.

This sea change within the Soviet system belies the accusation of "appeasement" levelled by some conservatives against the West's response to these changes. It is they, not we, who are in disarray. It is they, not we, who are making the substantial concessions. It is no exaggeration to say that they have lost the Cold War by forfeit. And if they have lost, we have won.

But what shall we do with this victory? What do we expect of the world, what do we want of the world, what role shall we—the sole remaining world power—play in

---

* *The National Interest,* no. 20 (Summer 1990).

the world, in this post–Cold War era? Our discussion (it is too early to call it a debate) of this issue is, to date, at a much more primitive level than the Soviets', as Sestanovich's article reveals. Even to mention "national interest" as a lodestar for American foreign policy excites controversy or revulsion. The Russians know that they have been deprived of the guiding principles of Soviet foreign policy, as established by the Bolshevik Revolution. We, the victors, are naturally inclined to think that our principles have been vindicated. But if one asks what these principles are, one gets a cacophony of responses. It isn't that we didn't know what we were doing this past half-century. It's just that we had so many good reasons for doing it. And these reasons, today, reveal themselves to be not only different from one another, but incompatible.

If one looks back at the basic principles—ideologies they may fairly be called—that have shaped American foreign policy since 1917, one can distinguish four that overlap and interweave, while always rubbing each other the wrong way. They are, in chronological order:

- Wilsonian liberal internationalism—a grand design for a new world order based on self-determination, nonaggression, conciliation and arbitration, and "collective security" ensured by a league of nations.

- A chastened and revised version of liberal internationalism, wherein the same ideal informed our rhetoric while the actualities of the Cold War shaped a modestly realistic policy of "containment." With the end of the Cold War, the rhetoric has moved to a unilateral emphasis on "enhancing democracy" abroad.

- Isolationism, of the Right and of the Left.

- A conception of the American "national interest," vague and inarticulate, but which nevertheless leads a kind of underground existence in our thinking.

Wilsonian liberal internationalism was based on the thesis that it would be possible to create a "world community" in which nations would subordinate national interests to the sovereignty of international law, as incarnated in such institutions as the League of Nations, the World Court, and a constellation of other, more specialized institutions (such as the International Labor Organization) that would cope with specific, narrowly defined problems. The league would not only pass judgment but would have the authority to enforce its rulings through the exercise of collective action, such as sanctions or even, if necessary, military intervention. In this vision, first elaborated two hundred years ago by Immanuel Kant, we would at last be moving toward world stability, world peace, and a "community of nations" whose shared values would make for a world order in which all nations would recognize the principles of self-determination of peoples and government by popular consent. The popularity of this point of view is best understood as a revulsion against the nationalist excesses that produced World War I, an especially ghastly war. But this popularity was both fragile and thin. Fragile because the spirit of nationalism, once reawakened, simply swept aside, as so many glittering cobwebs, the Wilsonian dream. Thin, because it took solid root only in the American State Department (and, to a much lesser extent, in some other foreign offices) while never being taken seriously by the overwhelming majority of the American people (or, it should be said, of any other people).

By the 1930s, this conception of American foreign policy had established itself so firmly in our State Department and in the minds of our policy-making elites—the Council on Foreign Relations being a noteworthy example—that even though the league was by now discredited for reasons of ineptitude, and the American people were moving massively into an isolationist mood, the Roosevelt administration could think of no other principles with which to fashion its foreign policy. After World War II, the United Nations replaced the League of Nations, but otherwise nothing much changed.

The post–World War II goals of American foreign policy, as officially stated, were Wilsonian. They seemed to represent the only mode of thought within which the American government has found it possible to explain its policies, and to a large degree the Cold War itself was interpreted and described in Wilsonian terms. We were the leader of "the free world," as well as of an anticommunist coalition of nations whose goal was the "containment" of communist messianism. The tensions this often involved us in turned out to be fatal. Thus, we fought a war "against aggression" in Korea, a war conducted under the aegis of the United Nations. It was also a limited, defensive war of "containment" that simply sought, at great cost, a reversion to the *status quo ante*. The American people soon made it clear that they did not like this kind of war—a fact soon forgotten (or haughtily dismissed) by our policy makers. So we ended up fighting exactly the same kind of war in Vietnam, only this time without success. By the end of that war the American people had, in effect, disengaged themselves from any Wilsonian national purpose, while "containment" itself was tainted with the hue of defeat. Fortunately, it turned out that "containment" had done its work even while many Americans were getting weary of it.

In the years between those two wars, however, the American people and their foreign-policy makers were—or seemed to be—largely in agreement. In a sense, American foreign policy in this period had two distinct strands—the rhetorical and the pragmatic. When President Truman announced his doctrine in 1947, he did so in familiar Wilsonian terms. The policy it inaugurated, however, was the "containment" of communist expansion through the use of American economic and military power. The American people supported this foreign policy because they despised communism as an ideology and were outraged by communist expansionism. The rhetoric they regarded as—well, just the kind of official rhetoric normally exuded by our State Department. In short, they felt involved in the Cold War *as Americans,* not as a leader of "the free world"—an abstraction that never meant much to them. Wilsonian ideals, indeed, meant nothing to them. The profound distrust that the American people felt toward the League of Nations has been transferred to the United Nations—an organization not simply futile but one that, more often than not, has exhibited a clear anti-American bias. Both Daniel Patrick Moynihan and Jeane Kirkpatrick became national heroes by giving eloquent expression to this distrust.

American policy makers shrewdly adapted to this reality. Their liberal internationalism gradually became less international, more unilateral, even more nationalist. One heard less—and hears less today—about a community of nations living tranquilly under international law, and more about our commitment to the "enhancement of democracy around the world." As the Cold War has come to an end, this remains the dominant, official motif of American foreign policy. It has appeal not only to liberals but to many conservatives who are ideologically adrift in the post–Cold

War era. From anticommunism to pro–"democratic capitalism" is a tempting move for those who wish to remain engaged in world politics.

This is, of course, a uniquely American idea, one that even our democratic allies in NATO, or out of NATO (for example, Japan), do not share. Their conception of the Wilsonian ideal has, in any case, always been more cynical—perhaps one should say "realistic"—than ours, in that they have never permitted their internationalism to override their specific national interests. They do believe in using international forums and international organizations to defend those interests—which is why the State Department finds them to be such faithless allies at the United Nations. None of the European democracies thinks it an important part of its foreign policy to "enhance democracy" all over the world. None of these democracies thinks of itself as "a city on a hill," as we do, having a special moral-political mission in the world, as we habitually think we do. Indeed, the very strength of this post–Cold War current of thought is its ability to tap the springs of American nationalism and American moralism, fused in a sense of *the* "American mission" or *the* "American purpose."

The inspirational rhetoric in which this foreign policy is clothed is itself so peculiarly and parochially American—no other nation talks about foreign policy this way—that one is bound to be skeptical of its viability. It may move Americans, but certainly not foreigners. Besides, it is Wilsonian enough to run into all the older Wilsonian dilemmas—dilemmas resulting from the disjunction between ideal and reality, general principles and particular issues. For instance, there is the issue of "self-determination," a Wilsonian principle that our State Department will never, never disavow—but will ignore if convenient. We are silent about self-determination in Kashmir, but outspoken about the right to self-determination of the Palestinians on the West Bank. One picks and chooses, while "holding firm" to the principle.

The case of Lithuania revealed starkly this unprincipled deployment of principle. Since we have never recognized the Soviet annexation of Lithuania under the Nazi–Soviet pact, there seemed to be a good case for recognizing the newly established government in Soviet-occupied Lithuania. Such a case was argued enthusiastically by those who wished to see us "enhance democracy" wherever possible. But it turned out that our Western European allies, along with the newly liberated nations of Eastern Europe, all vehemently opposed any such action. They saw no point, at this time and in these circumstances, in engendering a crisis in our (and their) relations with the Soviet Union over an issue that, compared with other things at stake, was marginal. There can be little doubt that the State Department and the White House were of the same opinion—but they couldn't figure out how to say so. So they hemmed and hawed and vacillated, showing weakness and indecision when, in truth, none existed. Such is the disadvantage of defining foreign policy in unequivocal moralistic-idealistic terms. It leads to an endless series of self-debilitating equivocations. In any case, how do we go about "enhancing democracy" where we do have freedom of action? One now hears—revived from the intellectual dead, as it were—much talk of the importance of "economic aid." One would have thought that the myth of economic aid, as an effective adjunct to foreign policy, was by now utterly discredited. In fact, it is. We know that, except in very special, and usually temporary, circumstances, economic aid does nothing to "enhance democracy" abroad. It feeds corruption, economic inefficiency, and political irresponsibility. The evidence leading to this conclusion is so overwhelming that it cannot even be called controversial.

So why are people, who not only ought to know better but do, suddenly so enamored of the idea? The reason is obvious: They cannot think of anything else to do. They dare not contemplate, much less raise, the prospect of American military intervention and occupation to "make democracy work" in friendly countries where it is in danger of collapse—in short, to create something like an American empire with a purely ideological motive power. This was never a serious possibility, and now that the Soviets have realized how futile it is, it is not and cannot be a serious option for American foreign policy.

True, one cannot object to the cluster of very small-scale programs that are being recommended to "enhance democracy" here or there or anywhere—supplying countries, for example, with "expertise" in everything from sewer construction to prenatal care. No harm in that—but no visible gain, either, so far as foreign policy is concerned.

One swift question ought to be enough to reveal the ultimate hollowness of this mode of thought: What shall we do about the Philippines? Here, after all, is a country with which we have had a long and intimate association. We understand this country better than we understand most others, and they understand us reasonably well. It also happens to be a country whose democracy we have helped establish and sustain. Nevertheless, that democracy is floundering and seems headed for disintegration. So what should we do about it? To ask the question is to provoke an echo, not an answer.

When a nation has played a leading role in world affairs for more than half a century, doing nothing comes hard.

The futility of a foreign policy whose purpose is to "enhance democracy" abroad is apparent to most Americans, and so the end of the Cold War has led to a resurgence of an isolationist temper. Among a handful of conservative thinkers this has led to a recrudescence of pre–World War II isolationism, a vein of thought streaked with nativism, chauvinism, and an unassuaged hostility to Franklin D. Roosevelt and the New Deal as well as to America's involvement in World War II, an involvement they attribute to a liberal conspiracy. There is also a handful of liberals (overrepresented in Congress) whose isolationism (though they would vigorously deny the title) derives from the desire to spend the maximum amount of money on social programs at home and the minimum abroad. In general, sections of the political Left, in all countries, display this predisposition. The Left has always tended to regard foreign affairs as a wicked distraction from its noble efforts to create a "better world," beginning at home.

Though these two currents of isolationism will often coincide over specific issues of policy—such as the stationing of several hundred thousand American troops in Europe—the tenor of their thinking is radically different. Right-wing isolationism is nationalist, left-wing isolationism is antinationalist. (They violently disagree on the permissibility of flag-burning and the importance of a large military establishment.) And because of this difference, right-wing isolationists are sometimes prepared to use military force against a foreign government that engages in actions hostile to the United States, while the Left would prefer to ignore it, or make some purely symbolic gesture. (The differential responses to our bombing of Libya come to mind.) There was a time when the Right was firmly attached to the Monroe Doctrine, so that its isolationism was actually hemispheric rather than national. This is less true today, but the benign reaction of the Right to the invasion of Panama, while the Left was disconcerted, suggests that something of this traditional attitude still survives. It is also obvious in the disparity of sentiments toward Castro's Cuba.

Both right-wing and left-wing isolationism aim to exploit an instinctual isolationism, almost nonpolitical in character, that has always pervaded American opinion. George Washington's admonition against "foreign entanglements" remains engraved in American hearts, so that every such "foreign entanglement"—World War I, World War II, Vietnam—however enthusiastically endorsed originally out of a sense of patriotism and pride, is followed by an isolationist revulsion. It was the Cold War, in which our "foreign entanglements" were understood as necessary to prevent a communist takeover of the world, that permitted our policy makers, operating in the liberal-internationalist mode, to multiply such "entanglements," and to convince themselves that this mode of foreign policy would continue for the indefinite, perhaps permanent, future. But the end of the Cold War has changed all that. Our State Department may still believe that a strong, visible "American presence" in Europe is essential to "stability" on that continent. But it is increasingly difficult to make sense of such vague rhetoric. Our troops in Europe have been there to resist a Soviet invasion. If there is to be no invasion, why are they there? Not, one assumes, to intervene in case of "instability" in Eastern Europe, or Yugoslavia, or even the Soviet Union itself. If such intervention is necessary, surely our Western European allies can cope with it on their own.

And if quarrels erupt among those allies, whose side are we to intervene on? It is the inability of our official foreign policy to cope with such direct, "naive" questions that is giving impetus to an isolationist revival, on the Right as on the Left, in the United States.

Isolationism today has a bad name, largely deserved, because some of its more prominent spokesmen, especially on the Right, evoke echoes of the 1930s—echoes of nativism and xenophobia, indifference (or worse) to Nazism and fascism, broad hints of anti-Semitism. One forgets that in the 1930s there were perfectly decent spokesmen for isolationism, especially on the Left, notably Norman Thomas and the remnants of the old Progressive movement. Their case had been put eloquently by Macaulay in 1845:

> I do not say that we ought to prefer the happiness of one particular society to the happiness of mankind; but I say that, by exerting ourselves to promote the happiness of the society with which we are most nearly connected, and with which we are best acquainted, we shall do more to promote the happiness of mankind than by busying ourselves about matters which we do not fully understand, and cannot efficiently control.

This "little England" approach to British foreign policy, though not at all unpopular, was nevertheless swept away by events, as Britain engaged in competitive empire-building in order to retain its status as a world power—indeed, at the time as *the* world power. One can predict with much confidence that a version of American isolationism will suffer the same fate. In a way, we have no real choice, any more than Britain did. A great power is as much responsible for what it does *not* do, yet is in its power to do, as for what it does. Power breeds responsibilities. Britain had no *British* reason to use its supreme naval power to suppress the international slave trade, in which the British had not been involved for many decades. Under existing international law, it didn't even have the authority to do so. Nevertheless, it used its navy for exactly that purpose, for no better reason than that such an action defined the *kind of* great power Britain would be. It was a matter of national identity, not of foreign policy in any strict sense of the term. One cannot easily divorce the foreign policy of a superpower from its very national identity.

So the United States does not really have the option of withdrawing into a "Fortress America." Not only does the degree of our integration in the world economy today make this economically impossible—our prosperity cannot be separated from the relatively unrestricted movement of goods and investments—but the American people are not about to relinquish their position as a world power. That would go against the American grain, against the sense that Americans have of their historic destiny. It would be like demanding of Americans that they be indifferent to the performance of American athletes in the Olympics—or that we hold a kind of minor-league Olympics of our own. That is psychologically unthinkable. You don't hear American sports fans chanting "We're number two!" or "We're number three!" But if both the old and the new liberal internationalism are bankrupt, and if isolationism is a nostalgic fantasy, where does that leave American foreign policy? It is at this point that the idea of constructing a foreign policy in terms of our "national interest" gains credibility.

The notion of an American "national interest" is not a new one, and has a perfectly respectable history—until it was swamped and discredited by the liberal-international mode of thought propagated by Woodrow Wilson. Throughout the nineteenth century, the term was freely and casually used here, as it was in Europe. After all, George Washington and Alexander Hamilton and James Monroe had established its propriety, and no American thought it strange to be informed by elected officials, or by journalists and publicists, that some particular action was or was not in our national interest. After the Wilsonian revolution in American foreign policy, however, it was felt that we no longer had a national interest in having a national interest. The term and the idea were associated with either a reactionary parochial isolationism or a ruthlessly amoral realpolitik. Even to talk about "realism" in foreign policy was regarded as suspect—as it still is today in many circles.

It was, of course, Vietnam that dealt a mortal blow to liberal internationalism. As has been noted, the unpopularity of the Korean War should have transmitted a warning signal that the prescribed role of the United States, as defined by our commitment to the United Nations Charter, was not something the American people felt at all comfortable with. But the intensity of the Cold War in the ensuing years, and the natural hostility of these same people to communism and communist expansionism, served to obscure this unease. After Vietnam, no president could echo John F. Kennedy's rhetoric about "our" willingness to endure any sacrifice in order to "deter aggression." Liberal internationalism remained the orthodoxy in our State Department, but the American people were leaving that church in droves.

Ironically, it was the Left, in its opposition to the Vietnam War, that breathed new life into the idea of "national interest." Much of the Left, of course, was oriented only to an anti-anticommunist foreign policy that merged into a traditional kind of left-wing isolationism. But there were scholars and writers on the Left who, seizing upon the writings of Hans J. Morgenthau and George F. Kennan, did revive the concept of the "national interest"—though, lacking the vestiges of a nationalist instinct, they didn't know quite what to do with it. It is only today, in the post–Cold War era, that some conservatives, finding anti-communism no longer a useful compass with which to orient themselves in world politics, and with the kind of nationalist bent that has always been natural to conservatives, are trying to envisage an American foreign policy that is defined in "national interest" terms.

It is no easy task. Traditionally, national interest is defined in terms of plain military security or maintaining a "balance of power" among nations that are potential enemies or actual competitors for world status. But the United States has no reason to be concerned about its military security, so long as it retains a nuclear capability that nullifies the threat—for the moment, and one suspects for the foreseeable future as well, a minimal threat—of a hostile nuclear attack. And as the sole remaining superpower, there is no "balance" for us to worry about. True, there are theorists who would happily burden us with the mission of monitoring and maintaining a "balance of power" among *other* nations, large and small, in Europe, the Middle East, Asia, and elsewhere. This would make the United States the "world's policeman" for the status quo, or at least the world's arbiter for all changes in the status quo. Imagine the United States accepting responsibility for the fate of Kashmir and for "enforcing the peace" between India and Pakistan! We are simply not going to be that kind of imperial power. Perhaps a future historian will decide we should have been. But it is not to be, because ours is a democracy and the American people violently reject any such scenario.

Where, then, do we look to find a national interest? Well, history has seen to it that we do not begin with a *tabula rasa,* and the contours of such a definition are given to us by the realities we confront. Let me suggest the following principles that can serve as guidelines.

It is in our national interest that no other superpower emerge whose political and social values are profoundly hostile to our own. To put it another way: We did not win the Cold War against Marxist-Leninist messianism in order to tolerate, yet again, any comparable confrontation. As things now stand, there is no visible threat of any such superpower emerging. But history has not come to an end and is still pregnant with surprise.

It follows that it is in our national interest that those nations which largely share our political principles and social values should be protected from those that do not. As Edmund Burke wrote more than two centuries ago, "Nothing is so strong a tie of amity between nation and nation as correspondence in law, customs, manners and *habits* of life. They have more than the force of treaties in themselves. They are obligations written in the heart."

The United States enters the post–Cold War world with standing attachments and commitments. NATO may be an anachronism—I think it is—but we are not about to isolate ourselves from our fellow democracies in Western Europe, the Pacific, or the Middle East. Just how strong that attachment is, and how strong that commitment will be, will depend on circumstances—which, as Burke also pointed out, is the governing force in all policy making.

Our relations with the other nations of the world will be decided candidly on a case-by-case basis. Now that the "Second World" has, to all intents and purposes, ceased to exist, and along with it the category of "nonaligned nations," there is no other basis on which to operate. To the degree that any of these nations has a foreign policy friendly toward us, we will surely be disposed to be friendly to it. To the degree that it displays hostility, we will reciprocate. Similarly, to the degree that any country adapts its socio-economic-political arrangements to correspond to those prevailing in "the West," we will find it easier to be more intimate in our friendship. To the degree that it does not, our relations will be, at best, cool and correct.

There is no general formula that enables us to arrive at easy conclusions in any particular case. If there were such a formula, we could run our foreign policy by computer, feeding it such ambiguous concepts as "self-determination" or "aggression" and triumphantly announcing the results.

But what about the moral dimension of American foreign policy? It has always been there and, since we are an untraditional nation founded on a liberal creed, it always will be there. Have we nothing "higher" to offer the world?

Perhaps we do—though, with every passing year, I become less convinced. When some foreign political scientist or politician asks what books to read so as to discover the secret of our success, I find that I can think only of books by long-dead authors, many of them unread by Americans today. And when they consult American constitutional lawyers on how to go about writing a new constitution, I tremble for their future. It is these same lawyers, for the most part, who are busy rewriting our own constitution so as to rob it of its original merits.

Nor am I thrilled to observe the sweeping popularity of American popular culture throughout the world. I wish it were a lot less popular here at home, since it seems to me to be so recklessly subversive of the traditional ethos on which this democracy was founded and for so long sustained. We all talk easily about "values" today, but who today speaks for "virtue" as our forefathers once did? Even I find myself tongue-tied before that term.

Despite all such reservations, however, we are a successful nation—no question about it—and the envy of much of the world. It is perfectly understandable, therefore, that Americans believe we are still "a standing monument and example" to the world (to quote that brilliant rhetorician and much-inflated statesman, Thomas Jefferson). But what, precisely, does a "standing monument" do? Our isolationist tradition would have it just stand there, a role model (as we would now say) for the world to emulate. But the American people are of an activist temperament, which is why, as we became a "standing monument" that is also a world power, it has been so easy for a concern for universal "human rights" to grab hold of our imagination.

This concern was first elaborated, in its present form, in opposition to communist totalitarianism, which deprived human beings of all rights—deprived them, in fact, of their humanity. The apocalyptic vision of Orwell's *1984* provided us with the key text. But, in the course of the 1950s and 1960s, the issue was seized by the Left and used as a club with which to batter the moral legitimacy of anti-communism in general and of American foreign policy specifically. The strategy employed was to revise the conception of "human rights" so as to include, as human rights, the civil rights and civil liberties that are to be found in a modern liberal democracy. Since many of our allies in the Cold War were not particularly respectful of such rights and such liberties, we became vulnerable to the accusation of using a "double standard," one for communist regimes and another for noncommunist or (especially) anticommunist regimes. Today, this revision of the original idea of "human rights" is so orthodox that liberals and conservatives alike find themselves imprisoned in it.

But this blithely ignores the fact that there are large areas of the world which do not share our conception of civil rights and civil liberties, and are unlikely to move toward any such commonality in the foreseeable future. Saudi Arabia, for instance, does not permit Christians or Jews to become citizens or even permanent residents. Are we to allow this fact to disrupt our relations with that very important and relatively friendly country? Are we to contemplate the religious reformation of Saudi Arabia? No, we are not.

The truth is that, not only does our foreign policy have a double standard with regard to what is now called "human rights," but we have a triple and quadruple standard as well. Indeed, *we have as many standards as circumstances require—which is as it should be.* We react more cautiously to China's antiliberalization than we would to Russia's because our ally, Japan, whose interest in China is considerably greater than our own, has strongly urged such caution upon us. There is nothing "immoral" about such deference. We are free to engage in the quiet diplomacy of persuasion, the open diplomacy of intimidation, a foreign policy that may or may not involve military intervention—always depending on circumstance. If a Pol Pot regime were to be reestablished in

Cambodia and reinstitute its genocidal policies, we would surely break off diplomatic and commercial relations. But we would limit our response to that level. Should such a Pol Pot emerge in Cuba, on the other hand, we would almost surely intervene militarily. The reason for this disparity is that our interest in Cuba is radically different from our interest in Cambodia.

All in all, it is perfectly possible to envisage a post–Cold War foreign policy for the United States which, constantly defining (even redefining) our "national interest" as the world changes (and as we change, too), would be sensible and realistic. It would disburden itself of the incubus of liberal internationalism, with its utopian expectations and legalistic cast of mind. It would not be, could not be isolationist—unless, that is, one identifies the abandonment of liberal internationalism as *ipso facto* "isolationist." It would be realistic without being a species of brutal realpolitik—itself a special theory of international relations, originating in a special period of European history, that has no relevance to the American position in the world today or to the predispositions of our democracy. Obviously, such a foreign policy will have plenty of room for failures as well as successes. But both failure and success would flow from errors of judgment, not from illusions about the world and the people (including Americans) who inhabit it.

Will we move toward such a foreign policy? It is hard to see what other direction there is for us to move in. But it would be much better for us and for the world if this movement were clear-sighted, rather than if (as is all too likely) we marched backward into our future, constantly troubled by nostalgic intellectual loyalties and inappropriate paroxysms of self-doubt.

7

A WIN–WIN GAME

ROBERT L. BARTLEY

The elites who formulated the policy of containment in the late 1940s recognized the paramount trend of their time: the emergence of the totalitarian state, represented by a communist Soviet Union as well as Nazi Germany. They understood that this was a threat to mankind generally and to our own national security. They formulated a realistic and patient policy, and after two generations and despite occasional missteps, it seems to have succeeded. In 1989, the communist empire started to crack from within, as containment predicted. We cannot entirely dismiss the possibility that the ongoing revolution in Russia will throw up its own Bonaparte, but for now we can hope that the Cold War has been won.

As this hope is redeemed, we need to ask, what will be the character of the emerging era? Is there a new paramount trend affecting our security and well-being? I think the answer is clear: Over the rest of our lifetimes, we will live through a second industrial revolution. As the steam engine transformed an agricultural economy into an industrial economy, the computer is transforming the industrial economy into an information economy. Economically, this represents an enormous opportunity. Diplomatically, it means the emergence of an interconnected, integrated, interdependent world order. These developments will of course have their own frictions, but in general the trend is benign; our policies should facilitate it. Attempts to resist it will squander opportunity and sour both international relations and the domestic mood.

The emerging world order is not driven by the heady idealism of Dumbarton Oaks, but by economic and technological reality. Already, the economies of the nations are linked by twenty-four-hour financial markets. With nearly instant communication, the peoples of the world will increasingly be bound together. And it is becoming clear that, Orwell's fears to the contrary, permeating communications empowers not the state but the individual.

This was manifestly evident, indeed, in the miracle year of 1989. The communist Chinese leaders found that to suppress a student uprising in Tiananmen Square, they first had to confront Dan Rather. This did not keep them from shooting their way to continued power, but it did complicate their problems, raise their costs, and cast enormous doubt over their ultimate success. All Mikhail Gorbachev's intercontinental missiles could not impose his will on Eastern Europe, and probably in the long run not even on Lithuania. Even some new Bonaparte would face the same problems; how long could he sustain a gulag for millions of former communist party members? And with Russian, or

Chinese, elites plugged into the world, dissent would merely start all over again. In Albert Wohlstetter's phrase, "The fax shall make you free."

If the new era emerges as we hope, our national purpose will be to build international institutions appropriate to the order waiting to be born, and to manage the frictions it will create. This surely does not mean creating a new United Nations or other world-government-at-a-stroke. But it may very well mean a broader application of the slow, step-by-step, economics-first evolution toward unity we are already witnessing in the European Community.

Internationally, the first big step would be a new Bretton Woods—formalization of the exchange-rate stabilization implicit in the G-5, G-7 accords of the Plaza and Louvre meetings. The volatility of exchange rates opens and closes factories and destroys and creates jobs in ways that appear arbitrary, and indeed are. This creates enormous friction and pressures for protectionism. It would also be helpful if institutions could be designed or redirected to bring market economics to bear on the development of the Third World, and where possible to help nations, like Mexico, that have embarked on that course.

Militarily, the Soviet Union still holds a massive nuclear capacity, so deterrence will remain necessary in most foreseeable futures. If ultimately the end of the Cold War means the end of the threat of nuclear catastrophe, an integrated world economy would still require the historic military mission of suppressing piracy. When pirates come the size of Saddam Hussein, this will require international efforts, but the United States will still have to lead the way. A prison sentence for a German businessman selling poison-gas equipment is surely a hopeful sign.

But it is at home that America, and its elites, can make their biggest contribution to forging the new world order. If the whole world is about to become a melting pot, where else should it look for lessons or leadership? Similarly, it is America that has the history and experience of federation, presumably the future of Europe and perhaps even larger areas.

This above all means America must be true to its historic principles. It must strive to keep its markets free domestically and open internationally. Similarly, American immigration policies should be generous, by no means solely for altruistic reasons, but to keep our own society vibrant and young. It should strive to make its own economy "competitive," not to beat foreigners, but to make its best contribution to world prosperity.

It is appropriate for the United States to maintain diplomatic pressure against residues of mercantilism in nations such as Japan, but America should remember the patience behind its containment success. Mercantilist governments basically exploit their own citizens, and these policies too will be unsustainable in an information age. The main lesson for elites to teach, and learn, is that unlike military competition, economic competition is a win–win game.

These lessons sound trite, but they may not prove easy to implement. Ironically, the information age seems also likely to produce a rebirth of nationalism. Centrifugal tendencies are growing, in all likelihood precisely because nationhood has become less important. If there is free trade with the United States, Quebec does not need English Canada. In the end it may not matter, but in the medium term these trends can be destructive. American elites should seek to dampen American chauvinism, not to arouse it. If America seeks to resist the new world trend, to retreat into an isolated, inward-looking redoubt, the biggest casualty will be the American spirit. A newly isolationist America would be out of step with history, fighting a losing game, and watching other nations build a new world—in many ways based on American inspiration and American traditions but ironically without America.

Even now, the "decline of America" neurosis that has seized our elites stands in stark contrast to the optimistic, present-at-the-creation mood evident in the elites of nations of the European Community. Only five years ago the whole continent was sunk in Euro-sclerosis. But by adopting old-fashioned American notions such as privatization, entrepreneurial spirit, cuts in super-high marginal tax rates, and movement toward monetary union, Europe got itself into step with the emerging world trend. The United States can, should, and—after the current hesitation and debate—will do the same.

8

AN INDEPENDENT COURSE

TED GALEN CARPENTER

The sudden collapse of the Soviet Union's Eastern European empire at the end of the 1980s seems to have been nearly as traumatic for members of the Cold War foreign policy elite in the West as it was for Leninist true believers the world over. American policy experts who had grown accustomed to viewing global developments through a Cold War prism for more than four decades are now having to confront entirely new issues and contemplate a markedly different role for the United States. For the most part, they have not made the intellectual adjustment. In the months since the opening of the Berlin Wall, there has instead been a frantic search for new rationales and alternative missions to justify the perpetuation of Cold War policies and institutions.

Underlying such efforts is the assumption that although the Cold War may be ending, the United States must continue to play an activist role—especially a security leadership role—throughout the world. Michael Mandelbaum of the Council on Foreign Relations was only a little more candid than most of his colleagues in expressing that view when he told Thomas Friedman of the *New York Times* that although the Cold War is over, "We can't just pick up our chips. We have to stay at the table and get involved in a new game."

That is a distressingly myopic approach. Instead of reflexively clinging to a strategy of global interventionism, U.S. leaders need to define an entirely new role for the United States in a post–Cold War world. America must position itself to take advantage of opportunities that may arise from the breakdown of the bipolar Cold War system while avoiding the pitfalls that are also likely to emerge in what will be a more diverse and, at times, disorderly global environment. What is needed is a policy of strategic independence—an independent course free from the dangerous and expensive burdens of obsolete security commitments.

Several principles should guide that new strategy. Perhaps the most essential is that policy makers must overcome the belief that America lacks the luxury of choice, that it must continue to play the role of Atlas, carrying all the world's security burdens on its shoulders. That attitude is a product of the early years of the Cold War when the global balance of power lay in ruins and the United States seemed to be the only nation that possessed the economic and military strength to thwart Soviet (or more broadly, communist) expansionism. Today the assumption that only a U.S.–dominated network of alliances can prevent global catastrophe represents egregiously retrograde thinking.

Several major centers of power have emerged or re-emerged over the last forty years. The nations of Western Europe long ago ceased to be war-ravaged waifs incapable of defending the security of the continent. Japan now has the world's second largest economy and is capable of playing a more active political and military role in the Far East. China, India, and other nations have become significant regional actors with their own political, economic, and security agendas. Not only does the United States no longer have to police the planet, it is increasingly unlikely that it can do so without intruding on the interests of other powers, thereby creating needless frictions and confrontations.

A related principle is that in a post–Cold War world, U.S. leaders must learn to define American interests, especially security interests, with greater precision. Throughout the Cold War, there was a tendency to define "vital interests" far too broadly and casually—with the vast overcommitment to Vietnam as the quintessential example. The concept of vital interests should be reserved for those geopolitical assets that have a direct, immediate, and substantial connection with America's physical survival, its political independence, and the preservation of its domestic freedom.

Not all adverse developments in the world automatically impinge on vital American interests, thereby becoming national security imperatives that justify the use of force. Indeed, in a post–Cold War setting there may be many local or regional quarrels that are—or at least should be—of little relevance to the United States. It will require a major conceptual adjustment to restrain the interventionist impulses of policy makers who have been accustomed to viewing even the most obscure conflicts as possible Soviet expansionist probes carried out by political surrogates.

There is a danger that the United States will inject itself into such imbroglios even if the Cold War rationale for doing so no longer applies. The Bush administration's obsession with preventing "instability" in the world is especially ominous. It seems intent, for example, on converting

NATO from an anti-Soviet alliance into an arrangement with the amorphous objective of preserving European stability. That approach creates a multitude of unwarranted risks. The ethnic cauldron of Eastern Europe in particular may well be a prolific source of future conflicts. It was one thing for the United States to risk war to prevent the Soviet domination of Europe (however improbable that danger seems in retrospect); it is quite another to undertake such risks to suppress a struggle between Hungary and Romania over the status of Transylvania, or to curtail ethnic bloodletting among newly independent components of the Yugoslavian federation. The stakes simply do not justify the expenditure of American resources or the sacrifice of American lives.

Instead of regarding local conflicts as matters of wider concern involving the United States, Washington should seek to avoid such entanglements. That objective would require America to phase out its system of alliances. Even during the Cold War, alliances had become, in Earl C. Ravenal's apt phrase, "transmission belts for war," converting otherwise minor conflicts into potential superpower confrontations. Indeed, both the United States and the Soviet Union have frequently found themselves in the midst of quarrels between clients, usually involving issues that were at most of marginal relevance to the patrons. The tense confrontations between India and Pakistan, Syria and Israel, and the two Koreas are examples. The prospect of being drawn into unwanted and unnecessary conflicts by irresponsible clients will persist in the post–Cold War era. At the same time, without the Cold War rivalry even the most theoretical benefits to the United States of maintaining patron–client relationships will recede to the vanishing point.

An effective post–Cold War strategy for the United States would involve a more limited definition of vital security interests and the adoption of a more independent approach to world affairs. The shedding of alliance burdens could reduce America's defense costs by nearly two-thirds, producing a sizable peace dividend for the American people. Even more important, a policy of strategic independence would materially reduce the level of risk in what promises to be a dangerous and disorderly world.

The third principle that should guide American policy makers is that the necessary curtailing of security commitments must not lead to a headlong plunge into economic autarky or intolerant nationalism. The proliferation of protectionist trade proposals, the hostility to foreign investment in the United States, the drive for more restrictive immigration laws, and the ugly tone of many alliance "burden-sharing" debates show that the danger of such insularity is not imaginary. It is both possible and desirable for America to play active economic, cultural, and diplomatic roles in the world without being the planetary gendarme, and it is essential for the people of the United States to make that crucial distinction. The challenge for American leaders will be to avoid the extremes of either the promiscuous interventionism that has characterized U.S. policy since World War II, or the storm-shelter isolationism that immediately preceded it.

Ironically, many of those who seek to preserve the strategy of compulsive global activism are employing arguments that could eventually play into the hands of chauvinists and advocates of economic autarky. Secretary of Defense Richard Cheney, for example, insists that "the United States needs a military presence in Europe to maintain political ties with

Western Europe."* That is a crabbed view of America's influence, measuring it in only the most narrow military terms. Such reasoning fails to take into account the weight of the common democratic heritage, extensive cultural links, and pervasive economic ties between the United States and Europe. It demeans both the Europeans and ourselves to argue that estrangement will automatically occur without a large U.S. troop presence on the continent.

The notion that unless the United States virtually occupies a region militarily it cannot have productive economic and diplomatic ties with the nations there is fallacious. Other countries, most notably Japan, have been able to establish such ties without an overbearing military presence, and America did so throughout most of its history. Americans must relearn how to operate in a multipolar environment.

In fact, the United States enjoys some enviable advantages in a multipolar world. Unlike other major powers, it does not have large, potentially hostile neighbors. Its security problems are therefore less pressing than those of Japan, China, the Soviet Union, and the nations of Western Europe. America's economy is by far the world's largest, and with the manifest failure of centralized planning in the communist bloc as well as the Third World, societies around the world are looking with renewed interest at the free-market values that have made that prosperity possible. Likewise, America's political values are a source of considerable influence. From Tiananmen Square to the Berlin Wall, those who sought to bring a greater measure of freedom to their societies openly cited the American example of individual rights and limited government.

*New York Times, February 13, 1990.

It is essential that a post–Cold War strategy contain an element of idealism as well as a more rigorous, realistic assessment of America's security interests—as important as the latter may be. Throughout the history of the Republic, most Americans have wanted their nation to stand for enduring principles, not merely practice a calculating realpolitik. It is that subtle but important point that Patrick J. Buchanan (Chapter 3) and other advocates of a conservative national approach to world affairs fail to comprehend.

The challenge for policy makers in the 1990s is to formulate a strategy that leaves room for the promotion of values without embarking on an interventionist binge that will entangle the United States in dangerous and unnecessary conflicts. Long ago, John Quincy Adams made the correct distinction when he stressed that America "is the well-wisher to the freedom and independence of all. She is the champion and vindicator only of her own." A policy of strategic independence would make that same distinction in a post–Cold War setting. It would reserve the use of military force for the defense of vital American security interests while emphasizing the potent example of America's economic and political values. Such a strategy offers the best hope for minimizing the risks and maximizing the opportunities for America in the emerging multipolar international system.

9

OF VICTORY AND DEFICITS

STEPHEN J. SOLARZ

We are witnesses to an extraordinary moment in human history. The Berlin Wall has crumbled. The Warsaw Pact has collapsed. The Red Army has been driven out of Afghanistan. From Stettin in the Baltic to Trieste in the Adriatic, the iron curtain that so cruelly divided East from West has at last ascended.

In one Eastern European country after another, crypto-Stalinist dictatorships are being transformed into genuine parliamentary democracies. Even in the Soviet Union itself we are observing the gradual emergence of a multiparty system and the ineluctable dissolution of the last of the great empires.

We are on the verge of a nuclear arms reduction agreement that will reduce by half the number of nuclear weapons that threaten our continued existence on this earth. We are close to closure on a European conventional forces agreement that will entirely eliminate the huge advantage in conventional forces enjoyed by the Soviet Union and its Warsaw Pact allies. In short, although vestiges remain, the Cold War is over.

But the end of the Cold War, while a major achievement, does not mean that we no longer face any threats to the vital interests of our country. Stated simply, the main challenge to our national security in the twenty-first century is economic competition from Japan, a united Germany, an integrated Europe, and even the newly industrialized countries of Asia—especially the so-called four tigers of East Asia: Hong Kong, Singapore, Taiwan, and South Korea.

This challenge is manifested in our appalling trade deficit, which reached $108 billion in 1989. It is reflected in our abysmal rate of savings, which has plummeted to a deplorably low 2.5 percent of GNP. It is illustrated by our stagnant standard of living, which has seen the median family income, measured in real terms, remain virtually unchanged since 1973. And it is manifested in the escalating size of the federal debt, which has more than tripled since 1980, and which during the past decade transformed the United States from the world's largest creditor to its largest debtor.

These gloomy macro-economic trends are a reflection of some dangerous and depressing social developments. For instance, one out of every five children in America lives in poverty. Ten babies die in the United States for every thousand live births—a shamefully high infant mortality rate that places us behind eighteen other countries around the world. One American adult in four is functionally illiterate, whereas in Germany, Japan, and South Korea, adult literacy is close to 99 percent. Nearly 29 percent of all U.S. high school students leave school before graduating, compared with a dropout rate in Japan of little more than 1 percent.

Similarly, much of the physical infrastructure of our nation is outmoded or overburdened, which further reduces our capacity to turn back competition from overseas. Thirty-five percent of the country's interstate highway system has outlived its design life, while gridlock is increasingly the rule rather than the exception not only on our highways but at our airports as well. More than 40 percent of the nation's bridges are structurally deficient or functionally obsolete. In short, it is not too much to say that we are now moving into a world where the major threat to our national values will come not from the Red Army or the Warsaw Pact, but from economic competition from abroad and social problems here at home.

In earlier centuries, countries whose military might and standard of living made them world powers—Spain and Portugal in the sixteenth century, the Netherlands in the seventeenth, France in the eighteenth, Great Britain in the nineteenth—gradually slipped from the pinnacle of power into a shabby second-class status. The real challenge that confronts America is: Can we maintain our economic preeminence, or shall we, as did these other once-great countries, begin a long slow slide into stagnation, eventually to be eclipsed by other nations better able to meet the challenge of the technological age in which we live? Or to state this in slightly different terms, can we muster the will and marshall the resources to address these challenges in order to remain the wealthiest, most powerful, most envied nation in the world?

I believe we can. More to the point, I believe we must. But if we are to retain our place of preeminence, we will have to come to grips with the federal budget deficit, which stood at $152 billion in 1989. Already, interest on the national debt represents the most rapidly growing component of the federal budget. Totalling $180 billion in 1989, the amount we paid in interest was more than eight times the total budget of the Department of Education. Indeed, the immense size of the deficit is perhaps the single most important factor in eroding our nation's economic power and capacity to compete, since the deficit drains money otherwise available for economically productive investment and requires the Federal Reserve to keep interest rates artificially high. How can we hope to compete with the Japanese when our prime interest rate stands at 10 percent, while the comparable figure in Tokyo is customarily 2 to 4 percentage points lower? Reducing the size of the deficit in a prudent and expeditious fashion will produce a higher rate of savings, lower interest rates, and ultimately increased industrial productivity.

But it would be a profound mistake to believe that the only problem we have is the budget deficit. It is equally important that we deal with the social deficit as well. What those now engaged in hammering out next year's budget ought to be looking at is not simply a one-year decrease in the budget deficit, but a five-year program to reduce the deficit substantially, revitalize our human resources, and rebuild our physical infrastructure.

All of this, of course, will cost money—lots of it. A comprehensive plan to address these problems will cost as much as $600 billion over the next five years.

Much of this money can and should come from the defense budget. As we have seen, the end of the Cold War and the dramatic reduction in the threat posed by Warsaw Pact forces should allow us to safely make major reductions in military spending, thereby freeing up resources for investing in our country's human and physical capital while simultaneously getting the deficit down to more manageable proportions.

Of course, America will need to remain militarily strong. In an unsafe and uncertain world, threats of a military nature may still emerge. Unilateral disarmament is no more an option today than it was at the height of the Cold War. But given the diminution of the Soviet challenge, it certainly should be possible to eliminate systems and forces designed to deal with a threat that no longer poses the danger to our national security it did only a few years ago.

Let us not fool ourselves, however. A program designed to maintain our preeminence in the world cannot be funded by the defense budget alone. Already there are almost as many claims on the "peace dividend" as there are customers at McDonald's in Moscow.

Ultimately, dealing with the human and physical needs of our nation will require a significant increase in government revenues. As a practical matter, that won't happen unless there is a bipartisan agreement between the White House and the leadership of both parties in Congress. And without such agreement, it will be possible neither to substantially reduce the deficit, nor to provide the resources necessary to rebuild our country's human and physical capital.

To be sure, the economic future of the United States will depend primarily on the efforts and energies and entrepreneurial creativity of the private sector, which is responsible for 83 percent of our country's jobs, and which produces 80 percent of the GNP of the United States. But there are some problems—revitalizing our educational system, for instance, or rebuilding our infrastructure—that the private sector alone cannot solve. And unless we make resources available from the public sector, these needs will not be adequately addressed, and the private sector will be held back.

Of course we should not for a moment think that we can solve the problems facing our nation just by throwing money at them. All too often in the past, we simply assumed that providing resources automatically guaranteed results. Now we know better. It will be essential, therefore, to link the provision of any additional resources to strict performance standards, in order to make sure we get our money's worth. For the fact of the matter is that unless we can show a tangible return on our investment, political support for additional expenditures will evaporate.

Over the past two hundred years—little more than the tick of a second hand on the clock of history—we have accomplished many good and great things. We have stood for fundamental human values of decency, justice, and fair play. We have nourished freedom at home and nurtured it abroad. We have been generous in sharing our bounty with those less fortunate than ourselves. We have achieved a level of affluence undreamed of by our ancestors and unparalleled in the annals of mankind.

That, however, is the past. We cannot afford—now above all—simply to sit back and rest on our laurels. At the moment that we celebrate the collapse of communism and the triumph of democracy, we must also remember that the failure of communism has not meant that capitalism has eliminated all our social ills at home. Capitalism has made the American economy the envy of the world. But the "magic of the marketplace" will not, by itself, solve the problems of adult illiteracy, of fatherless families, of chronic unemployment. Capitalism, as dynamic as it has been, as robust as it can be, will not, on its own accord, repair our bridges, unclog our roads, or unfoul our environment.

This, then, is both a moment of national celebration and of national challenge. For more than two centuries—indeed, ever since the first European settlers set foot on the shores of the New World nearly four hundred years ago—

Americans have kept alive the American dream. For generation after generation they nourished the belief that their children would enjoy a better life and a higher standard of living than they did.

Now this comfortable assumption, this American dream, has been called into question. Let us not be the generation that says we can no longer guarantee the American dream for our children. Let us not be the generation that gives up the sense of optimism and achievement that has made the United States the great nation it is today. Let us, instead, forthrightly recognize the new nature of the challenges to America's well-being. And having done so, let us once more summon up the will, the courage, and—above all—the vision to pass on to the next generation, and the next, and the next, the hope and the promise that has so richly blessed our own.

10

THE ULTIMATE HIGH GROUND

MALCOLM WALLOP

It is not at all certain whether the Cold War is truly over, or merely entering a more subtle and dangerous phase. But regardless of external conditions, America's purpose in an ever-changing world remains constant: to preserve the union, establish justice, insure domestic tranquility, provide for the common defense, promote the general welfare, and secure the blessings of liberty for ourselves and our posterity.

I believe the American idea was divinely inspired. It is God's antidote to man's unlimited ingenuity in finding ways to oppress and enslave his fellow man. America is the only society in history established expressly as an alternative to despotism, to allow the maximum liberty within a framework of public order. In standing for liberty and justice, America stands for something beyond itself, for liberty and justice are the ends of decent men and women at all times and all places. What is unique in history is the existence of a particular country devoted to these universal ends.

As long as it continues to embody these ideals, America is worth preserving at all costs. But such a nation, whose very existence is both a constant reproach and an alternative to oppression, will always be threatened, for the thirst for the power to enslave his fellow beings flows naturally from the heart of man. It is a natural consequence of that ancient temptation, old as man himself, that "ye shall be as God"— autonomous and accountable to no one or nothing except one's own desires. Communism is merely one of the most clever and persistent forms of the lamentable human tendency to despotism. But it will not be the last. Human nature is immutable, and there will always be aggressor nations and nations which fall prey to the aggressor.

Nations, like all else in nature, cannot remain static. They are either on the pathway of growth and strength and maturation, or they are stagnating and regressing. Some people think a nation can stop its development at some chosen point, or perhaps move sideways. This delusion merely obscures the true course of such movement, which is decline.

The United States has grown and matured into a world leader—and not merely a leader, but a force in the world for positive good. As a result, we have a responsibility first and above all to our own liberty and independence, but to an extent also to the rest of the world. Can a great nation simply shrug off its responsibilities? How do we feel about a father who deserts his children, or a policeman who ignores a cry for help? This is not to suggest that the United States should be a father to mankind or the world's policeman. But, inescapably, we do have responsibilities as a world power that we cannot lay aside without paying a severe penalty as a people and as a nation. Failure to meet responsibilities inevitably exacts a harsh penalty, even if the consequences are not immediately evident.

The irony is that today, in response to the dramatic changes shaking the world, many conservatives—some of whom I admire immensely—have joined the Left in calling for retrenchment from the world. The call of the Left to "Come Home, America" now has an echo from the Right. The Old Right rejects the global interventionism or world-wide crusade for democracy of Charles Krauthammer and Ben J. Wattenberg (see Chapters 1 and 11, respectively). But "neo-imperialism" or "neo-isolationism" constitutes a *false dichotomy*. There are other avenues open to us.

I agree with my colleagues on the Right that our first duty is to America's liberty, particularly now that it is under an insidious domestic assault potentially as destructive as the threat from Marxism-Leninism. The former victims of Soviet imperialism are struggling to free themselves of state control over mind, movement, intervention, and all the suffocating remnants of socialism. Yet at the same time, our politicians, the media, and academic elites are advocating them for us. We have to resist this siren song at all costs if there is to be a future America worthy of a national purpose.

But our fight for a renewed American polity must not become an excuse for turning totally inward, for showing our backs to our allies, for ignoring vital interests which do lie outside our borders whether we like it or not. Such retrenchment can be as stifling to national purpose as creeping socialism, and I must oppose it. It is simply another form of fatal stasis, an embrace of irresponsibility, an impossible autarky that means inevitable decline.

In my view, there are three broad goals that together constitute our national purpose in the post–Cold War era. But to carry out any national purpose, we first have to understand and commit ourselves to this proposition: Foreign policy and military posture must be synchronized. A foreign policy without the military power to assert it is emasculated. And a huge, costly military posture without a foreign policy rationale is insupportable in our present democracy. But if we can harmonize the two, then we can achieve our goals.

First, *secure the victory* over Marxism-Leninism. We must make sure the dramatic changes in the Soviet Union result in a society that does not and cannot threaten the West, and that the process is not reversible. This is an extraordinarily difficult alchemy—changing the base metal of a moribund Marxist-Leninist empire into the gold of free, democratic societies. And although the Left perversely rejects this notion, we have little influence over the process. But by maintaining our military strength, by keeping up Solzhenitsyn's "Wall of Resolve," we can perhaps ensure that the transmogrification of the hostile system continues, and block its return to aggression and imperialism.

Second, *sustain free-market and democratic forces.* To paraphrase John Quincy Adams, we are the friends of liberty everywhere, but guardians of only our own. We do not meddle in every dispute, impose our form of government on alien cultures, or play midwife to every embryonic movement around the world that calls itself democratic. But when conditions are right, when our help is needed and sought, we have a responsibility, an obligation as a friend of liberty, to sustain those fighting for freedom, remembering that our own struggle for independence could not have succeeded without outside help. If we cannot bring ourselves to do this much, then we cannot call ourselves the "friend" of liberty, and our liberty simply becomes an expression of selfishness, not a blessing shared.

Patrick J. Buchanan's litmus test of a legitimate national purpose is "Are Americans willing to fight for it?" (Chapter 3). But if this test becomes the standard of leadership when liberty is at stake, then opinion polls become the criterion by which decisions are made. And without firm, enlightened, principled leadership, America will follow the polls into permanent decline.

Third, *pursue our interests*—as *we* define them—the first of which is security and survival. This means we must remain engaged in the world, confident, not aggressive, but retaining the initiative—the ability to act on behalf of our vital interests how, when, and where we choose.

Simple geography compels us to remain engaged and active outside our own borders. We are an island continent and a great maritime power. At present, we depend primarily upon the seas for life-sustaining trade, for access to foreign markets, energy sources, and raw materials. It is a military imperative—a sea power must have bases and friendly ports around the world, a network of allies. Ships need to be repaired and refitted, stores replenished, crews rested, and all must be protected. "Good armies have good friends," said Machiavelli. The same may be said of good navies. Without them—without our active engagement worldwide—our strategic depth and reach would extend only a few days' steaming from our own shores.

But simply meeting the limited external requirements to support our sea power is not enough. Contrary to the Krauthammer thesis, there is no assurance that the future will produce a hegemonic world order friendly to America or our ideals of liberty. The final chapter is not written on socialism. We have plenty of experience with capitalist nations turning to Marxist socialism, but no experience with the reverse. The return to democracy is not assured, and in any case will not be without intense struggle. Socialist states, while groping for freedom, may even try to alleviate the pain of the transition by asking the capitalist West to shoulder the cost of their failed programs and policies, and draw *us* deeper into the socialist morass. It strains credulity to think the socialist paradigm will be undone in favor of some worldwide consortium of capitalist democracies whose policies will be compatible with our interests.

Rather than attempt to orchestrate such an unlikely policy, I would prefer to see us concentrate on making U.S. sovereignty so unchallengeable, and the U.S. economy so dynamic and competitive, that we would never be drawn into a supranational world order. The beguiling notes of "one-worldism" are in essence a cry of despair, a lament that nation states and the *particularity* that people everywhere cherish are somehow obstacles to freedom and prosperity. But the opposite is true. We must continue to move forward into the future full of hope, affirming our identity, our principles, and our unique heritage.

To be forward looking in this era is to be *upward* looking. To continue to grow as a nation no longer demands expanding outward on land and sea, but upward into space. I am convinced we cannot achieve these three broad national goals without two things—the strategic defense of the United States, and mastery of space.

Space is not merely one vital factor of U.S. security. Space control, or at the very least assured access to space and unrestricted freedom to operate in it, are *indistinguishable* from our long-term national security and prosperity, for two reasons.

First, space is the ultimate strategic high ground, the "terrain" from which conflicts of the future may be determined. We are embarking on a new "Revolution in

Military Affairs," an era when traditional ideas of war-fighting must yield to the dominance of new high-technologies and the importance of military assets in space. Already our terrestrial forces, whether army, navy, or air force, rely heavily upon space for surveillance and intelligence, navigation, command, control, and communications. In many ways the crucial military leverage is shifting to space in such a way that space control may determine the course of events on the ground without a shot ever being fired by terrestrial forces.

The Soviets clearly understand the strategic dominance of space, and have a vigorous military space doctrine coupled with a formidable operational capability. They may well believe that a military monopoly in space is the one thing that could salvage the dramatic unraveling of the Soviet empire. Certainly they believe that denying it to us assures their continued presence as a superpower on the world's stage.

If Gorbachev or some resurgent Stalinist leader should decide reform has gone far enough, or if the USSR acquires a sufficient transfusion of trade, credits, hard currency, and Western technology to resuscitate their dying empire, then a Soviet monopoly in space could reverse the supposedly irreversible process.

I can envision a future scenario in which the Soviets could checkmate us from the ultimate high ground, in keeping with their doctrine of victory without war. They would be able to dictate terms, to coerce us "peacefully" into submission. If they can control the ultimate high ground of space, and have the confidence that their intercontinental ballistic missiles—space weapons, by the way—can strike targets without hindrance, then it matters little who rules Poland or East Germany. Their dominance and leverage would be global, and their diplomacy would reflect it. Soviet military control of space would enable them to engage in a new type of strategic intimidation, with the possibility of a more subtle but more powerful form of coercion than is possible even with traditional nuclear strike forces.

Conversely, to deny the Soviets the ability to blackmail us from space is one way to secure the victory which has begun, and ensure that the "Evil Empire" changes irrevocably into a nonthreatening confederation of democratic states or independent nations.

This is the real significance of the Strategic Defense Initiative. Strategic defenses will counter the military utility and blackmail potential of the Soviets' ICBM arsenal and first-strike capability, or that of a third nation or terrorist regime. Furthermore, a vigorous SDI program will produce far more than simply missile defense. The technologies and operational capabilities flowing from SDI, the tremendous breakthroughs in sensors, miniaturization, and high-speed computers for example, and the anticipated development of cheap, reliable space-lift, all suggest that strategic defense can be the cutting edge of U.S. dominance in space, while at the same time reducing the threat of ballistic missiles. And the domestic impact of the technological advance will assure us economic competitiveness as well.

Second, space is also the great high seas of the future. It is the new frontier, with unique properties that will make possible forms of human endeavor generating wealth and benefits to mankind that we can now only begin to imagine, and make the United States truly competitive with the rising economic centers of Europe and the Pacific. In the sixteenth and seventeenth centuries, the nations that learned to exploit the new frontier of the high seas prospered. Spain, Holland, and England in particular became great nations because they were *seafaring* nations. In the same way, the great nations of the future will be the *spacefaring* nations.

Space will prove to be increasingly essential for communications, data-handling, and transportation. It will generate new forms of products manufactured in near-zero gravity, new minerals mined on the surface of the moon and asteroids, and an inexhaustible source of energy. The list of possibilities is endless.

I also believe the challenge of space will lift the eyes of Americans, inspiring them with new dreams and new horizons. Our mastery of space will direct the entire national sensibility upward, draw prosperity along with it, and surround us with security. Without lofty horizons, our sense of national purpose atrophies. And when national purpose withers, transcendent goals degenerate into self-interest; the nation stops growing and moving forward; it looks to government for comforting solutions, even for meaning; and freedom dies.

I will not say that it is our Manifest Destiny to plant the flag of freedom and human dignity on distant planets. It has been over twenty years since we raised our flag on the moon, and in many ways we have turned our backs to that momentous achievement. It is entirely possible that we will flinch at the challenge of space, turn inward, and slough off our responsibilities as a great power. That is certainly a course of action we might choose, either actively or by default. But the high ground of space is where the United States may renew its strength, and find new national purpose. Mankind benefited immeasurably from the exploration of the New World. Americans benefited immeasurably from the settlement of the Western frontier.

The same benefits are available in space if we will reach upward for them. After all, "a man's reach should exceed his grasp, or what's a heaven for?"

II

NEO–MANIFEST DESTINARIANISM

BEN J. WATTENBERG

I f, once again, the problem is the American Purpose, I offer this solution: neo–manifest destinarianism.

It makes sense, and it is much more fun than the alternatives. The Academic Declinists, with Paul Kennedy as brigadier, say America's purpose is to manage its decline gracefully. How thrilling. The Declinists are wrong when they say America will no longer be Number One, but more important, and less noticed, is the implicit notion that they don't want America to be Number One.

The Isolationists are led by Patrick J. Buchanan. Writing in this volume, Buchanan says American foreign policy should only be in the American national interest. How original. Buchanan says we should "come home" forthwith and stop already with this romantic democracy stuff. But doesn't the spread of democracy enhance our national interest?

Charles Krauthammer, also writing in this volume, and Joseph Nye, in his book *Bound To Lead,** make much more sense than either the Declinists or the Isolationists. Both know that America is and will be "Number One." They see that we must remain the major global actor. But for what American purpose?

Krauthammer envisions a "unipolar" world, explains that unipolarism means "the conscious depreciation not only of American sovereignty, but of the notion of sovereignty generally," and understands how difficult this would be politically. Nye says America should aim at "managing transnational interdependence" (MTI), and says that we reach the blessed state of MTI through the acronym soup: GATT, IMF, NPT, IEA, IAEA.

All right. But, again, toward what end? Why shouldn't America go for the gold? Which brings us to neo–manifest destinarianism.

Surely, America ought to wage democracy. But we ought never forget that there are many chambers in the palace of democracy. We ought to wage democracy generally, and democracy American-style specifically.

Democracy American-style is a way of life as well as a political system. It is not the same as the democracy of Japan, Inc. Nor is it the same as the stultified Swedish-style democracy. And yet, in Eastern Europe today, one important school of thought says the newly liberated countries should go Swedish. This doesn't seem to seriously stimulate Declinists, Isolationists, Unipolarists, or Transnationalists.

American taxpayers didn't put up trillions of dollars in the Cold War to create a few more Swedens. Not long ago Americans were troubled by the Swedish—read European—

*New York: Basic Books, 1990.

model. It was seen as decadent and even as "creeping so-cialism." Since then, they, and we, have gotten better. But differences remain. We might remember: Long before communism, the American revolutionary spirit was ad-dressed to providing an alternative to rigid European class-ism. There was a rich and fine fight between values of the New World and the Old. The "New's" were winning, and we still are. Now, with the totalitarians out of the way, we ought to kick it into overdrive.

If the world should evolve toward European-style so-cial democracy, or some democratic hybrid, or some uni-polar transnationalism, we can live with that. We and our allies will still have won a free world. But that result is merely acceptable. As the last superpower, we should try to shape evolution.

How can we do this? Let's back up and see where we are, and how we got to where we are.

Democracy won the World Series. In some large part this happened due to modern communications. The vic-tory was cultural and ideological; the weapons were in-formational.

That process will likely continue. In the future, the Number One country will be the one that is most success-ful in shaping the global democratic culture.

(The economic determinists—the Apocalyptic Bean Counters—are wrong when they say that Number Oneness will be determined by who makes the most semiconductors, or who gets the rent from an office building on K Street, although, in any event, America will continue to do very well economically. We still have, by far, the highest standard of living in the world, and the next time you hear about how ill-educated and un-innovative we are, you might remember that in the 1980s Americans won two-thirds of the Nobel

Prizes in science and medicine. By the way, does anyone re-member what the merchandise trade balance was of the Roman empire?)

Today, only the American democratic culture has legs. Only Americans have the sense of mission—and gall—to engage in benign, but energetic, global cultural advocacy. We are the only mythic nation, says Max Lerner. We stand partially guilty as charged by anti-Americans—we are the most potent cultural imperialists in history, although gen-erally constructive and noncoercive. (Neither the Romans, nor the Brits, nor the Dutch, had the ability to put a VCR tape in every village in the world.)

If communications of values is the key, how do we get fully engaged? Americans have always felt they had some-thing very special to offer. This sense of mission was once called Manifest Destiny. At times it did go overboard, into distant geographic expansion and wild-eyed cultural impe-rialism. We know now we can't clone the world American-style. And these days, any geographic expansion must be requested by the expandee, although there is direct dial from Canada to make things quicker.

With all the caveats, American democracy has distinc-tive features. Tocqueville had it right when he spoke of "American exceptionalism." (Indeed, it is now measured clearly in cross-national survey research.) Most Americans believe most of that exceptionalism is beneficial. Individu-alism, pluralism, opportunity, capitalism, upward mobil-ity, dynamism, and the absence of a rigid class structure come most quickly to mind.

We ought not be passive players. We have the sharp-est cultural arrows in the biggest quiver. These include our global entertainment monopoly, immigration, the spreading English language, the prime tourist destination, the best universities, the most powerful and far-flung military, an opportunity society, and a worldwide information operation.

There are things that government could actually do. There are conditions that government may only encourage. And there are areas the government should butt out of, letting nature take its course. Here are a few examples, big and small:

Our government cheapskate communication policy is penny-foolish and pound-foolish. Because of budget constraints, the Voice of America (VOA) recently publicly considered cutting language services. That may have been a Washington budget trick, but even its contemplation tells us more than we want to know about how we are conducting our public diplomacy.

Some budget-cutters say we should stop work on a new American shortwave transmitter, now under construction in Israel, designed to carry VOA and Radio Liberty into the Moslem areas of the USSR. The case is made that the Soviets are no longer our adversaries. Let's hope that's so. But won't the global uni-power (us) still have something to say to the sixty million Moslems of Central Asia, when Moslems are the fastest growing, and most volatile, segment of the world's population?

Luckily, American values are mostly spread by nongovernmental means. But shouldn't the government, when possible, encourage such enterprises?

All commerce is not of equal value in the contest for the culture. The export of computer chips is important. But more important is that American television programs and movies have fair access in other countries, that the English language spreads, that it is easier for tourists, teachers, and students to come to America.

The global entertainment business is dominated by America. Yet, television programs and movies are not included in the General Agreement on Tariffs and Trade (GATT). That makes it difficult to keep foreign entertainment markets open and fair. But one reason entertainment is out of GATT is that Congress is under domestic pressure to keep the American maritime industry un-GATTed. That gives foreigners a case to keep entertainment out of GATT. Given our current circumstance, the box-office should have a higher priority than boats.

(The reach of the American cultural dominion is moving from incredible to awe-inspiring. When some California glitz-merchants held a trade show recently there was one unusual aspect: One billion people, in ninety-four countries, watched it on television!

Why? Because the California peddlers were selling American movies at the Academy Awards, and American movies—and television and music—are the only universal currency there is in the entertainment business. And getting stronger, as communications deregulate around the world, as the middle class grows everywhere, as the demand for products to put on the air grows geometrically.

Why so popular? Not because we have the best filmmakers, although we do. But because our films, even the left-wing, allegedly anti-American ones, reflect our style of life, and our style of life has a magnetic appeal to billions around the world.)

America is the number one tourist destination. People don't just gawk at Yosemite, the Empire State Building, and the Jefferson Memorial when they visit. Tourists soak up the flavor of the American experience and take it home. Yet of the free countries, we have the toughest visa requirements. Another example: Other nations subsidize hostels so that young foreigners can easily visit. We don't.

The American Federation of Teachers estimates that there are more than 50,000 teachers of Russian in the five Eastern European nations, but fewer than 5,000 teachers of all the Western languages put together. The Russian teachers are skilled instructors—but are now without students. Most of them would like to learn English, and teach it. Let them study in our universities. In return, they could teach American students about the nature of evil empires. More important, they could instruct the faculty on the same topic.

We also ought to make it easier for foreign students to study here. About two million per year want to. Only about 350,000 can afford to.

We also ought to help American universities set up branches in Eastern Europe. The Eastern Europeans know there is a difference between American-style university education and the credential-oriented intellectualoid European system. They want to see the difference first hand, and we can provide that easily. We ought to take in more legal immigrants. Among other things, they are the greatest global gossipers. They spread the word.

We need a much broader definition of the phrase "public diplomacy." We are engaged in an enterprise called "foreign policy." That enterprise has many aspects. These include military, diplomacy, intelligence, and that stepchild, "information." As the global circumstance changes, the mix of foreign-policy activity ought to change. Thankfully, we need fewer tanks and less covert intelligence. We need more information diplomacy, and we ought to use all the arrows in our quiver.

Why? Because that's what Americans do for a living, and it's not new stuff. On the back of the dollar bill you will find the Great Seal of the United States with the Latin words *Novus ordo seclorum*—"A new order for the ages." They are words as old as America and as fresh as tomorrow.

Remember this about American Purpose: A unipolar world is a good idea, if America is the uni.

12

A POPULIST POLICY

PAUL M. WEYRICH

The perceived end of the Cold War has, not surprisingly, precipitated a major foreign policy debate, the first serious one since the isolationists effectively surrendered to the internationalists in the aftermath of World War II. These essays have played a useful role in laying a number of alternatives out for discussion. However, they have also shown the essentially fictitious nature of most of the debate.

On the one hand, there are a number of commentators who want to continue playing the old internationalist game as if nothing had changed. The decline of the Soviet Union and the end of the Cold War simply give internationalism greater scope, in their view. The United States can set itself new, grander objectives, going beyond the mere containment of communism to establishing a unipolar world and even achieving Nirvana itself—a Pax Americana—*à la* the Francis Fukuyama thesis. All this will be done through the beneficent exercise of American power via the State

Department, the Pentagon, the government generally, and, overlying and underlying all, the Establishment.

On the other side is isolationism. Having triumphed over communism, we will simply pack our bags and return home from "over there" to turn our attention inward. In fact, while there are a few actual proponents of isolation, for the most part isolationism is itself a conjuring trick by the internationalists, a hoodoo they call up whenever they feel threatened. They like nothing better than suggesting that the only alternative to their preferred "finger-in-every-pie" internationalism is isolation. If they can make that the debate, they know they will win.

Isolationism is the internationalists' preferred opponent because it is obviously not in accord with the real world. Our economy is increasingly integrated into the world economy; when the Persian Gulf sneezes, we all catch cold, and when the Tokyo stock exchange falls, we worry if we will be able to sell the bonds to cover our Treasury's borrowing. We drive cars from Japan, sell our agricultural products to the Soviet Union, and, increasingly, work for companies owned overseas. To suggest we isolate ourselves from the rest of the world is to say we should somehow separate ourselves from what we produce and consume.

So, in this caricature of a debate, the internationalists carry the day. But on closer study, their prescription is no more in accord with reality than that of the isolationists. The fall of communism could be less significant in the long run than the rise of many other power centers, ranging from Europe and Japan through India and a resurgent Islam to the Latin American drug cartels. The United States will control a shrinking minority of the world's power in the twenty-first century. It will hardly be in a position to impose a Pax Americana.

Of equal importance, the internationalists' position does not accord with domestic political realities. The American public has never been comfortable with having us poke our nose into everything that happens around the world. It is getting decidedly weary of foreign aid, and sees little reason for us to station troops around the world if the Cold War is really over. Our form of government, with separation of powers, does not lend itself to a foreign policy detached from public opinion. Often, when Congress messes up the executive's grand foreign designs, designs dear to the internationalists, it is doing, perhaps unfortunately, what it was intended to do: reflect the popular will.

So does that bring us back to the isolationist position? No. Rather, it suggests we look beyond caricatures, to search for a real alternative to the internationalists' position.

That alternative begins to become visible when we realize that what the internationalists want is not merely U.S. engagement with the rest of the world, but a specific kind of engagement—engagement through government. Government is the Establishment's playing field, and it is understandable that they should want engagement on that field, because it allows them to control the game and be the major players in it. It also allows them to profit from it; a great part of the Establishment lives off the defense and foreign affairs game in general and the NATO game in particular. The threat the end of the Cold War poses for the latter concerns them gravely; they are in the position of fleas whose dog is dying.

But engagement need not be engagement through government. Only when we realize this do we begin to see the real alternative. What is that alternative? It is the policy we pursued through most of our history as a nation.

America was never isolationist or isolated; we were never Tokugawa Japan. Rather, through most of our history, we related very actively to the rest of the world, but not through actions by government. We did it through commerce and ideas.

America was active in international commerce right from the beginning. Even as a British colony, our economy was trans-Atlantic. From our inception as a nation, America also used ideas and ideals, especially the ideals of personal liberty and democracy, as channels to the rest of the world. What most distinguished both of these instruments from the usual diplomacy and military force was that they related not to governments, but directly to peoples. Ours was a populist grand strategy, in which the American people reached out directly to other peoples through their products, their markets, and the beliefs embodied in the American political system.

It was a powerful and active policy. The fact that it was driven by public beliefs and the independent vigor of a free market economy rather than the decision of a foreign ministry made it no less effective. Indeed, our official foreign policy was most effective when it sounded the same themes, as in Woodrow Wilson's Fourteen Points proposal. Such policies were powerful internationally because they resonated among the publics of other countries. They did so because of the image of America our populist strategy had generated in those countries.

This was far from an "isolationist" grand strategy. It was, in fact, internationalist in a highly sophisticated way. It was equally sophisticated domestically, in that it commanded broad, enduring public support because it was rooted more in private action than in government policy.

Is a return to a populist grand strategy a viable alternative to the strategy of playing the internationalists' game and engaging ourselves diplomatically and militarily in most of the world's events? Contrary to what the foreign policy establishment argues, a strong and legitimate case can be made that it is. The current and prospective international environment promises to make commerce and ideas more powerful forces than they were in the nineteenth century, and the strategy worked then. The world economy is just that, a transnational economy in which foreign trade plays a growing role in most nations' economic life. In much of the world, the free market is growing as socialism proves a dismal failure. Free markets offer increased opportunity for people-to-people relationships through commerce.

The international market in ideas is also growing by leaps and bounds, largely as a result of new information technologies. It is becoming increasingly difficult for authoritarian governments to keep unwelcome ideas out. The new means of transmitting ideas past old barriers offer great opportunities for the ideals America has always stood for—the ideals of liberty and democracy. Again, the trend can foster people-to-people relationships, the basis of a populist grand strategy.

All of this is not to suggest that we never have to use our military strength in this dangerous world. Indeed, there are times—precisely to protect the sort of commerce we are talking about or to assist those struggling for freedom—when it is not only appropriate but necessary.

A good example of the opportunities today's world offers to a populist grand strategy are those to be found in Central Europe and the Soviet Union. The peoples of those countries—not their governments, except as they follow the people—are throwing off the yokes of dictatorship and socialism. We can help them. We can help them best by sharing our experiences with democracy and a free market with them, so they can learn from our mistakes rather than having to make their own. But this cannot be done through their governments, which even in the best cases—Czechoslovakia and Poland—are still enmeshed with the Communist bureaucracy left over from the old regimes. It must be done on a people-to-people basis.

Over the past year, I have had the privilege of being personally involved in this sort of work in Hungary, Romania, and the Soviet Union. The contrast with my many experiences working with government—including our own—could not be greater. The democratic opposition in these countries is desperately eager to learn from us. And they do learn: In many years of teaching political techniques to groups of citizens, I have never found people more talented, more imaginative, more intelligent. They have a dedication to their countries and their futures that far surpasses what we see in American legislators—in part, no doubt, because none of the democratic officeholders in these countries is a professional politician.

In the course of this work, I have encountered other Americans doing the same things in these countries—teaching democracy and free enterprise, not just as ideas, but from a "how to" techniques standpoint. Some of them have been from the liberal Democratic side of the spectrum. But none of them has been from the Establishment, from the well-endowed, well-"careered" set. Why? Because the Establishment only knows how to act through government. And what has our government been doing in the face of this tremendous opportunity in the East? Government activities range from trying to perpetuate NATO to trying to keep

Gorbachev in power or discourage independence in Lithuania and other states controlled by the USSR.

Central Europe and the Soviet Union also illustrate the potential of a populist foreign policy in a reverse direction—in what we can learn from them. First, they can offer a definitive answer to the radical professors on so many of our campuses, who still rail at religion and Western culture and preach a socialist paradise. Let us make these radicals debate against people who can tell them what it is like to live in the kind of country they call for, a country where equality is the only virtue and traditional values are officially suppressed. Experience is a good answer to theory.

More broadly, we can learn from people who, despite severe repression, have held onto elements of our shared traditional culture, which we, in our consumer paradise, have let slip away. Religion is one such; it is no accident that the churches have played a major role in the collapse of communist governments. It is not impossible that a revival of religion in the West generally could come out of Russia and Central Europe. Similarly, while our culture has become a television culture, with all the decay that implies, theirs have remained literary cultures. Children still read the literary classics in school. Average citizens read books and listen to poetry. They discuss what the books mean. Literature, serious literature, plays a major role in their lives. Perhaps we can recapture that from them.

But none of this is happening or can happen through governments. It can only happen between peoples. Ultimately, which is more important to our long range future: the number of troops some treaty allows us to keep in Germany, or the flow of ideas about democracy and free enterprise into Central and Eastern Europe and the flow in return of ideas about man and God? Or, for that matter, the implications for our trade of a Central and Eastern Europe with open, expanding, dynamic economies? The answers are obvious. All contests, strategists have pointed out, are fought at three levels: moral, mental, and physical. Why should we continue only at the physical level when the moral option plays to our strength?

A populist foreign policy is what our Founding Fathers envisioned for us and championed. They were right then and they are right now. It is time for a foreign policy not just for America, but for Americans.

13

NOT TOO MUCH ZEAL, PLEASE

PEREGRINE WORSTHORNE

An American role in the world is not like God. If it does not exist, there is no need to invent it. Does one exist? For the immediate post–Cold War world, I rather doubt it. At any rate, not in the sense of there being some single new burden the American people have a moral duty to shoulder—a new manifest destiny. This does not mean that intellectuals—or even journalists—should not try to devise a new role, as they have in these essays. Certainly so far as I am concerned, the exercise has proved extremely useful, for the inadequacy of the answers so far has confirmed my hunch that nothing that can properly be called a role in the Achesonian sense—"Britain has lost an empire without finding a new role"—any longer exists or is likely to exist for many years to come.

The need for a foreign policy, of course, always exists. But a national role is a lot grander than a foreign policy. Containing the expansion of Russian power was a foreign policy. Containing the expansion of Russian communism was more like a role. By "role" Acheson meant a missionary foreign policy—something equivalent to the white man's burden. In that sense, Britain has not had a role these last forty years. I suspect that the United States would be wise to resign itself to the same perfectly bearable fate. But America, I will be told, is not Britain. Whereas it is possible for Britain to have a foreign policy without having a role, America needs a role to have a foreign policy. That is to say, without a moral purpose Uncle Sam won't be prepared to act abroad at all. I wonder. That the American people won't sustain over a long period the kind of enormous effort abroad required to win the Cold War, without a moral purpose—that is obviously true. But then neither would Britain or France, or any of the allies. It does not seem to me at all self-evident that Uncle Sam is so foolish as to suppose that the choice is always between going flat out on a foreign crusade or doing nothing abroad at all.

In any case, there simply is no great crusading cause around at the present time for the Americans to lead. What about the cause of democracy, some contributors to this volume ask. I trust those who propose the championship of democracy all over the world as a new American role are joking. Here I ought to declare an interest. My faith in democracy is very far from absolute. Most of Britain's important freedoms date from the pre-democratic age, and only very recently has Britain moved irreversibly away from aristocracy to democracy—with results that are by no means all to the good of the country. These are highly complex matters. Democracy has unquestionably proved a disaster in Africa, and Britain was very ill-advised to try to impose parliamentary government in areas where it had no chance of taking root. In Singapore, however, autocracy has proved very successful. Indeed, compared to so-called democratic Kenya, for example, so-called autocratic Singapore is much more civilized and prosperous—and even free. As for the countries of Eastern and Central Europe, should America really play a crucial role in deciding which particular form of government they eventually adopt? If the Hungarians and Romanians, say, want to restore their monarchies, is there any possible justification for the American influence to be thrown against such an attractively reactionary development?

I am not trying to be frivolous. There are horses for courses, and democracy is not necessarily the right horse for all courses. Presumably the American ideal is that all peoples should enjoy a system that brings them "the greatest happiness of the greatest number." In certain historical circumstances, that utilitarian ideal can just as easily be fulfilled by a despotism, a theocracy, or a military empire as by a free republic, just as regional peace and prosperity can just as easily be brought about through imperial rule as through national self-determination.

As Americans watch the dissolution of the Soviet empire they should remember what happens when empires collapse. Heaven knows this century has provided plenty of chastening examples. The case against imperial rule is that it lacks consent. Nobody ever asked Gauls or Jews or Britons whether they wanted to be part of the Roman empire; nor Indians and Africans and Malays whether they wanted to be ruled by Britain; nor Croats, Poles, and Moldavians whether they were happy to belong to the Hapsburg monarchy. What neither rulers nor ruled, however, fully grasped were the consequences of national liberation in terms of disruption and violence. For if the case against imperial rule is that it lacks consent, the case for it—

argued cogently in the *Sunday Telegraph* by Geoffrey Wheatcroft—is that it imposes stability, at least until its final hours. Quite apart from its function of holding different peoples apart who would otherwise be at each other's throats, great empires are usually too burdened with a vast administrative apparatus to be able to think of attacking their neighbors. Great wars stem from the unleashing of national passions—such as were unleashed by the French Revolution—rather than from imperial rivalries.

At the turn of the century, Europe was faced with a profound challenge not dissimilar from the one facing it now. It was called the Eastern Question and arose from the disintegration of the Ottoman empire. No satisfactory answer was ever found to the problem, which was why nineteenth-century British statesmen in their wisdom favored propping up the sick man of Europe, as Turkey was then called. World War I, which destroyed a generation, was the direct consequence of the failure of that policy. As a result of that war, not only was the Ottoman empire destroyed but so were the Romanov, Hapsburg, and Hohenzollern empires, in whose wake came the Bolshevik and National Socialist revolutions which exterminated millions and in turn led to World War II.

Supranational empires don't dissolve into a vacuum. They give way to succession states, ostensibly representing the principle of national self-determination; in practice usually more intolerant of their own minorities than the old empires had been and in any case puffed up with long-frustrated national pride. After 1945, none of these lessons was learned. Under American prodding, the Western European powers embarked upon another great bout of imperial dissolution—the decolonization of the maritime empires. As a result, Africa is now littered with impoverished successor states incapable of doing anything much more than oppressing their own peoples. Asia is torn by conflict between Hindus and Moslems, Tamil and Sinhalese with one successor state having been in the hands of a ruler, Pol Pot, whose crimes equal those of Hitler and Stalin. As for the Middle East, where Arab and Jew threaten mutual extermination, that, too, is an area which has suffered grievously from the so-called blessings of the end of empire.

Suffice it to say, then, that the end of empires need careful handling. Crudely handled, these historic processes can go disastrously wrong. The Baltic states today are very much a case in point, as are the Soviet Union's Central Asian republics. The American Congress would like to see Washington encourage today's independence movements within the Soviet empire with the same indiscriminate enthusiasm as it encouraged the independence movements within the British, French, and Dutch empires. President Bush, to his credit, has adopted a much more cautious and skeptical position, courageously refusing to allow public opinion to force him to make the same mistakes that were made by his predecessors, Woodrow Wilson after 1918 and Franklin Roosevelt, Harry Truman, and Dwight Eisenhower (remember Suez) after 1945. Perhaps the point that needs to be emphasized in this respect is that morality offers no clear idea to what should be done about the decay of empire. Certainly there is nothing for America here that could properly be called "a role"; nothing to set the Potomac on fire or provide a sense of crusading mission.

This does not mean that there will be no simple calls on American idealism. There will always be enough odious regimes, like that of Marcos in the Philippines or Noriega in Panama or Amin in Uganda, that can safely be overthrown by a righteous use of American power. But even in these cases I would prefer American intervention to be justified as a defense of civilization rather than as a defense of democracy (the two, unfortunately, are not always the same).

The Cold War simplified these difficult questions. For it could plausibly be argued that Russian communism constituted a uniquely evil challenge which required from the United States a uniquely virtuous response. Just as some kinds of infection are so awful as to justify the forcible quarantining of anyone suspected of harboring them, so there was one kind of political infection—communism—which justified the compulsory quarantining of any country suspected of falling victim to that terminal political sickness. Academics can now argue whether communism ever did constitute such a terminal sickness. What cannot be argued about, however, is that it made perfect sense to assume that it might have. Nor can it be doubted that the Russian superpower was dedicated to spreading this terminal virus over the world. So, during the Cold War, there was "a role" for the United States. Nothing of that order exists any longer. Not only is communism a crumbling ideology, but the Soviet Union is also a crumbling empire.

Am I suggesting, therefore, that the United States should withdraw into its own continent—return to its old policy of isolationism, as Patrick J. Buchanan recommends? Quite frankly, that seems to me a silly suggestion. Is it really supposed that the United States might wash its hands the fate of Israel, for example, or of South Africa? America's Jewish and black votes preclude isolationism in both these regions of the world. A protectionist fortress Europe would soon bring into play other equally powerful pressure groups calling for Washington to take some action or other. Then there is the not-so-little matter of terrorism.

Unless an isolationist America kept all its citizens within its own borders, there would undoubtedly be cases of Americans being murdered and kidnapped in foreign parts. Here again, public opinion, probably led by Mr. Buchanan, would call for American intervention.

U.S. noninvolvement in the world is no longer a serious option. But to be clear about this does not lead us any closer to the definition of anything resembling "a role." Where this inability to define a new "role" could be seriously damaging is in respect to European defense. For obviously only "a role" can begin to justify keeping 300,000 American servicemen on my side of the Atlantic. So much is indisputable. But might not a mere foreign policy be sufficient to justify the maintenance of a much smaller force?

Here I come to my only constructive suggestion. The end of the Cold War does not put an end to the need for some American presence in Europe. But it changes the justification for that presence. During the last forty years, the justification has been to keep the Russians out. In the next period the justification will be to keep the Germans down; or if not exactly down, at any rate not too triumphantly up. Pacifism is the new danger in Europe, not militarism. Above all, this is true of Germany. Germany wants to get rid of all soldiers from its soil and will happily give up its own if this means getting rid of other people's as well. The form German's revived nationalism is likely to take is anti-militaristic, neutralist, and pacifist, if only because the Western allies do not want it to go down any of these paths. Just as in the 1930s independence for Germany meant the freedom to rearm, in defiance of allied wishes, so now in the 1990s it means freedom to disarm, also in defiance of allied wishes; or at any rate Western allied wishes. Russian wishes will be another matter. Russia would welcome a disarmed Germany and possibly make the withdrawal of its own troops conditional on a neutralized Germany as well.

Of course, peace and the end of the Cold War are to be welcomed. But nothing is ever quite what it seems. It is through peace that Germany can now achieve the dominance of Europe. For in a disarmed Europe, East as well as West, where economic strength counts for everything, German economic power will carry all before it. So long as Western Europe was frightened by Russia, Britain and France (because of their nuclear armory) carried much clout. Now that NATO has officially made its declaration of peace, their prestige and influence will count for far less. Indeed, it can now only be a matter of time before Germany mounts pressure on them to renounce their nuclear weapons altogether as the price to be paid to keep Germany nonnuclear. Not only will the decline of Soviet strength favor Germany; so also will the decline of the military importance of Britain and France.

In my view the European Community has no serious chance of containing a resurgent Germany whose economic influence over both Eastern and Western Europe will soon lead to political influence as well. Without some external factors, the balance of power in Europe will soon become dangerously upset. An American military presence on British soil should be that balancing external factor. It need not be a large one; only really a token of American political involvement. Arguably, in the post–NATO period, France, too, would accept American bases. I see a British-French-American military alliance as being the successor to NATO with the purpose of maintaining some sort of European balance of power. Nothing more grandiose is going to work. For Europe in the next period will be in a state of flux, and it is idle to try to build any very solid or ambitious political edifice on such shifting sands. We are not talking about a new role for America so much as a holding operation while Europe, East and West, sorts itself out. For this purpose, Britain is America's ideal partner—antipacifist, anti-protectionist, and still basically pro-American.

Even when the Russian threat to Western Europe was at its height, there was little stomach for the fight in most of the Western European countries. Now that the Russian threat is thought to have disappeared, there will be even less. Pacifism will grow apace. Britain and France are the great exceptions to this European rule. In our two countries, the rot has not set in to anything like the same extent. In both cases the morale of the armed forces is exceptionally high. Some of the best and brightest of the young are eager to join. Whereas in most British institutions standards have fallen, in the armed forces they have risen. Where is willingness to die for one's country strongest in Europe?—undoubtedly in Britain and France. Germany, Scandinavia, the Low Countries, and even Italy may now be richer. But if there should ever again be a need for Europe to defend itself—against, say, a resurgent Islam—the only hope for effective action would lie with Britain and France.

Not too much zeal—that should be the motto for American foreign policy at the present time. The tides of history are running fast in the right direction. So only a light and delicate touch on the tiller is needed. Perhaps, for America, this is to ask the impossible. I don't believe it. For America, nothing is impossible.

14

A TIME FOR MODESTY

NATHAN GLAZER

There is a good deal of extravagance, to my mind, in the first two chapters in this volume, by Charles Krauthammer and Nathan Tarcov. Whatever other disagreements I may have with Patrick J. Buchanan, I find nothing objectionable in his flat assertion, "When this Cold War is over, America should come home." We should not be frightened by the word "isolationism." Context is all: The original isolationism demanded that the United States should do nothing in the face of a rising Nazism, that this was Europe's problem, not ours, and it added some considerations that turned out to be false, such as that an increase in military power to confront Nazism would lead to the decline of freedom in the United States itself.

Well, it certainly did have consequences—an enormous increase in the power and influence of central government in the United States. But on the whole, freedom has been well secured in the United States, better secured than in the period when military spending was a mere fraction of what it is today, and our military manpower numbered in hundreds of thousands rather than millions. The original isolationism also included a good dose of selfishness—let the world take care of its own problems—and a more suspicious dose of neutrality as between fascism and democracy. Indeed, in some isolationists, one suspected a positive preference for some aspects of fascism. Thus, isolationism had to be opposed.

But the main reason it had to be opposed by those concerned for the national interests of the United States was its indifference to the truly mad expansiveness of Nazism. The agonies suffered by Jews and socialists and communists under Nazism played hardly any role in getting us into war or guiding what we did once we were at war. Jews and those concerned for Jews had to press their case for a more activist American foreign policy in almost underground ways, rather than publicly. In those days, the only legitimate expectations in the way of a governmental response to Nazi persecution were such things as presidential statements or changes in trade arrangements—that was after all the model for American intervention in czarist Russia's persecution of Jews.

During the first eight years of Hitler's rule and the beginning of the war, the purpose of saving the Jews from vicious persecution would hardly have swung any weight in arguing for a military alliance with the enemies of Nazi Germany. Death camps might have been more persuasive, but we knew nothing of the plans to exterminate the Jews of Europe until late in the war. This was a unique event in world history; it would have justified almost any response. The fact is, however, that knowledge of the destruction of the Jews of Europe would have had little effect in a country then rather anti-

Semitic and much less inclined to intervene for human rights. Indeed, even after we knew about the death camps, immigration laws kept out the victims or potential victims of Nazism, even the smallest and most innocent.

It was the threat of Nazi expansion that brought us onto the world military stage. And the main reason American troops have been stationed in Europe and Asia since has been the fear of the expansiveness, and threat to our own security, of what remained in our minds until the late 1980s an apparently self-confident and aggressive communism. We were of course also committed to democracy, with varying degrees of commitment from successive American administrations. This was our way, and the way of the countries of Western Europe with which we most closely identified. But as we know, there were many divergences from support of democracy as we carried out our policies. Anticommunism came first in affecting our foreign policy, and from the point of view of our national security interests, that was correct: Authoritarian, nondemocratic regimes did not threaten us, nor did they possess the powerful ideological arms of Nazism and fascism in the 1930s, or of communism in the 1940s, 1950s, and 1960s.

Whatever our commitment to governments of freedom and democracy, it would never have justified the enormous expansion of American military power were it not for the threat of communism. The fact is that communism is now almost everywhere in disintegration, and that the part of it which truly represented a military threat—the Soviet Union—is unraveling, preoccupied with its own internal problems, and has lost as allies its subjected satellites in Eastern Europe. There is no longer a meaningful Warsaw Pact. One must ask why there is need any longer for a military alliance called NATO? One concludes that the only reason we seem committed is inertia. And so we continue to think of new nuclear missiles, and we remain committed to maintaining armies in Europe and Japan, bases around the world, and a huge military establishment proportionately twice the size of those of our allies, and which will decline, according to the Bush administration, only at a derisory 2 percent a year.

The arguments for the maintenance of such a policy seem to be a mix of empty words, not further analyzed, and of specific and particular considerations of one or another country which really should not centrally concern us. The isolationist Left and Right, Charles Krauthammer writes,

> ignore the indispensable role that the deployment of American power plays in the maintenance of global stability. There is nothing that would more destabilize Asia, for example, than the withdrawal of American troops from Japan. No country from South Korea to China to Thailand to Australia—not even Vietnam— fears the deployment of American troops. . . . Not that they expect immediate Japanese rearmament.

I find all this mystifying. Japan does not rearm *not* because American troops protect it or because our troops prevent a resurgence of Japanese militarism, but because the Japanese find it a good thing to get along without a huge military establishment. And after all, it is *we* who keep encouraging them to strengthen their military forces.

There is, of course, always reason for small countries to fear large countries. To take an example, Canada and Mexico on occasion and for some purposes fear American power. Would that be an argument, had the world evolved differently, for some other great power (Japan?) to station armies permanently in the United States? And in view of the fact that Japanese relative economic power is enormous and grows apace, just when *does* a United States in relative economic decline get to withdraw its armies from Japan?

We hear even more of the need for American arms in Europe to defend "stability" there. The issue is no longer defense against the Soviet attack through Germany that was the original basis of NATO and NATO planning over these last four decades, even though that has seemed increasingly unlikely for the last twenty years. We now have more complex arguments for the American military presence: Poland will be frightened if Germany is not included in NATO, or if an American general is not in command of NATO forces. But why would anyone believe these tensions and fears are the prelude to destabilization and war? Almost all European nations are now democratic or becoming democratic, and there is a universal horror of war in democracies which have experienced major wars. Further, there is a universal desire for a better material life, which would be threatened by war. Is it reasonable to expect German military power to be exerted on Poland or Czechoslovakia? Azerbaijan and Armenia are near war, Hungary and Romania glare at each other, Lithuania may be crushed by Soviet forces—but what can an American army in Germany do about any of these conflicts? One can—as in the case of Japan—propose scenarios of a resurgence in militarism, with an inflamed Japan or Germany ready to reconquer lost territories, but that is so unlikely when one takes into account the mood of most Japanese and Germans as to be a very wispy basis for a foreign or military policy. (It is also an argument for *permanent* American military forces in Europe, for who knows when the scenario might not come into effect?)

True, their nuclear arsenal and ours still exist, and careful approaches to bringing them down remain necessary. But one is at a loss to see what role continued American military forces in Germany play in affecting that process.

Big countries with great economic power will inevitably carry weight, and that will be the case with Japan and Germany, but there is no role for American occupying forces, whether to restrain these countries or reassure their neighbors, in this inevitability. And the world does, after all, change. There is something like a fragmentary and evolving world order, which will evolve more effectively now that the formerly communist countries are joining the rest of democratic Europe. There is international law, the United Nations, the GATT process, and many other international institutions, and despite the growing strength of some countries and the continued weakness and poverty of many others, the former do not ride roughshod over the latter. Boundaries remain stable, the rich countries provide aid to the poor, they try to adopt trading rules which assist the poorer countries, and the like. The poorer countries have a moral claim rather than any force with which to pursue their interests. For a long time they did have the chance to threaten allying with one of the two great antagonists if the other did not provide aid, and that did shake loose a good deal of aid. But will aid end now that Russia is withdrawing from the competition?

Even if the great change that Francis Fukuyama discerns may be debated, lesser changes of significance in the relations among nations have occurred. Big, developed, democratic countries now engage in no or very small wars. Germans and Japanese have discovered that economic growth and competition bring greater rewards, and much safer ones, than big wars. England and France have learned that colonies are a headache and they do better without. The United States has learned that wars to maintain "stability," as in Vietnam, can be very expensive and domestically disruptive, and may be very hard to wage and win. We engage now only in very little and very safe (for us) wars—Grenada, Panama. Even regarding these, one may well ask, was this war necessary? I think not. Even little wars kill a lot of people. Our Panama adventure turned out to be very expensive, Panama is no better off, and American policy makers now undoubtedly wish they had not brought Noriega into the toils of the American system of justice, where he will demonstrate its incapacity, ineffectiveness, and fecklessness for years to come. (The Falklands involved a more substantial issue of principle.)

So then, what is America's purpose now that the Cold War is over? Are we to be simply a country like any other country? No country likes to think of itself that way, and certainly not one that is still for a time the greatest economic power in the world. Of course, as Nathan Tarcov tells us (Chapter 2), the United States "remains explicitly founded on universal principles of human equality, individual rights, government by consent, and the right of peoples to alter or abolish their governments when destructive of these ends." We are proud, and rightly so, that these principles are increasingly accepted as the right principles for the organization of governments and societies, that even African dictatorships now fumble their way to multiparty regimes.

What I find difficult to understand is why our promotion of these principles in the present-day world requires a great military establishment, with bases throughout the world. Admittedly, many specific issues remain to be worked out. Should there be an American military presence in South Korea? Do we need the huge bases in the Philippines? What do we do about an Israel surrounded by permanent enemies, and which takes the largest single country share of American aid? I would say there are varying commitments derived from history, from our own responsibility for certain problems, and from internal political pressures—none of these are to be fully denied. Military forces and commitments will remain: I speak about scale.

Some of these specific issues seem easier to resolve than others. Some are bedeviled by the nonsense of a Cold War that is disappearing. One is thus mystified as to why the United States is involved in bringing the Khmer Rouge back to power in Cambodia, and can only explain it as a leftover of the Cold War—and a very complicated and almost incomprehensible leftover at that. As well as one can figure it out, because Cambodia is ruled by a regime backed by communist Vietnam, we seem to think anything else is better, even the Khmer Rouge, because that is backed by the "good" communists (China), while Vietnam is backed by the "bad" communists (Soviet Russia), except that we now think better of the "bad" communists than the "good" communists, do we not? I will leave it to the foreign policy specialists to explain this and other follies; for example, the fact that we continue to back Pakistan, a country that was also backed by the formerly "good" communists, China, and which we hoped would oppose the "bad" communists, Russia. The reality was that the only thing that truly concerned Pakistan and the only country it would conceivably fight was India, which had resorted to the "bad" communists, Russia, to get arms because we were supplying arms to *their* permanent enemy, Pakistan.

One has the strong feeling that these and other nonsensical American policies are simply leftovers of a Cold

War which is rapidly disintegrating and will be left to wither on the vine. But one is not so sure. Policies seem to have a way of surviving whatever reason justified them in the first place.

To return to America's purpose, it is not to become enmeshed in permanent alliances, whether based on the balance of power, some presumed geopolitical conflict, or an assumption of permanent and unchangeable ideological division. It is not to be the policeman of the world. George Washington was also a Founding Father, and his lasting heritage was the Farewell Address.

We should maintain our democracy and our commitment to free government. We should applaud, and, if we can, give aid to those who want to institute free government. We should show our disapproval of authoritarian, dictatorial, or totalitarian rule. Our direct weight and influence in making democracy and free economy the attractive things they now are in so much of the world has been limited: Our example has played a larger role. And this was all the Founding Fathers intended. They had no idea that one way we would promote our permanent commitment to those universal principles on which this country was founded would be to maintain armies around the world. These armies served their function in the age of expanding antidemocratic ideologies. It is hard to discern the emerging problems—and they are numerous indeed—against which American armies could be effective. In promoting and recommending those universal principles to which we are attached, it is now time to withdraw to something closer to the modest role that the Founding Fathers intended.

15

ENTANGLED FOREVER

JOSEF JOFFE

"If communism is dead," Irving Kristol pointed out to the 1990 gathering of the Committee for the Free World, "then anticommunism is dead, too." This is true in a way of a tautology—*per definitionem*. Alas, there is more than a vacuous truism to this proposition. For it puts the axe to the roots of almost half a century of American foreign policy.

Or does it?

Realpolitikers would fiercely deny such a lapidary DOA pronouncement. They would insist that anticommunism was but the icing on the cake, rich as it was. American foreign policy since 1945 has followed interest rather than ideology, and so the former will outlive the latter. Cut through the anticommunist clamor, they would contend, and you discern the classic behavior of a normal great power.

Their rebuttal might continue along these lines: The end of American innocence came as early as 1947—when Britain abdicated responsibility for embattled Greece.

With Stalin set on expansion, and Britain and France—both exhausted—out of the equation, the United States had to assume the burden of the balance for good. No longer could the United States withdraw behind the cozy barrier of the Atlantic (and the fog of idealist *pronunciamento*). Like the great powers of yore, America was now irrevocably stuck in the self-help system that is the essence of world politics, and so it had to obey the system's eternal rules. Which it did—consciously or not. True, the Truman Doctrine, the founding document, was enveloped in the grandiloquent oratory of antitotalitarianism. So were NATO, SEATO, et al., those Cold War alliances thrown up around the Soviet Union. But in essence, these were the time-honored tools of power politics—coalitions sponsored by the United States in order to constrain the one and only rival who threatened America's physical security.

Move and countermove, thrust and parry, became the choreography of a stylized, sometimes bloody "grand strategy" that Americans had always learned to despise as the game of princes and despots. But "containment" was the same game nonetheless. Whether it came to coalition-building (as in NATO) or coalition war (as in Korea), whether the crisis was over Berlin or Cuba—all the way down to the Euromissile Battle of the 1980s—the United States acted as great powers have always done: so as to balance or best its existential foe.

By way of Q.E.D., our realpolitiker would conclude: The power of Soviet Russia and not the threat of communism was the motivating force of postwar American foreign policy. How else would we explain our long-term love affair with the communist despots of China, which even the Tiananmen massacre could not interrupt? How else would we explain our "policy of differentiation" in communist

Eastern Europe which ranged us along such sterling characters as Nicolae Ceausescu? Indeed, if the real game was value rather than balance, why did America fall into bed with a long succession of nasties from Chiang Kai-shek to Manuel Noriega (before he was fingered as a drug lord)?

If the realpolitikers are right, then all is not lost now that "communism is dead" and Mikhail Gorbachev is dragging his country into democracy and the free market. If Russian power rather than Soviet ideology is the problem, then America's purpose must still address itself to the great existential threat embodied by Moscow. Communism might disappear, but thermonuclear weapons and vast conventional forces will not. (Precisely for this reason, even a disintegrating Muscovite empire will pose the single most important danger for world stability and American security.) Russian democracy would change hardball into softball, but not the rules themselves (which, at any rate, must always take into account a reversion to yesterday's pitching and slugging). Alas, in spinning this tale, the realpolitiker has left out a critical part. Democracies do not like realpolitik, and none has disliked it more than America, the oldest democracy which was founded in revulsion against the "corrupt game of princes" that was Europe's bloody lot.

In their own minds, Americans never went to war to uphold the balance of power, let alone for glory or booty. What really riled them in their first war was the "Cruelty & Perfidy" of George III—above and beyond his "plundering our seas [and] ravaging our Coasts." When America at last entered the war against Germany in 1917 and 1941, the nation did not think about the European balance but about the sheer evil of Kaiser Bill and Adolf Hitler. Nor was Russian power the problem that galvanized American society during the Cold War; it was the *ideological* enemy as embodied in the persons of Stalin and his successors.

Writing about "Democracy in America," Tocqueville reminds us of the basic reason: "There are two things that a democratic people always will find very difficult—to begin a war and to end it." In other words: Democracies do worst in the twilight zone between war and peace. Unless they are roused by great passions or great ideologies, they turn their backs on "reason of state." Yet once they are so roused, they similarly ignore the subtle intricacies of diplomacy. Instead, they will fight to the bloody finish when the foe is at last crushed as prelude to his moral-political reform.

Indeed, reason of state or the "primacy of foreign policy" are fundamentally alien to the democratic spirit. They imply a realm of policy that is above and beyond the fray of democratic politics. If the people are the sovereign, *no* issue must be excluded from the public debate. The very idea of the "primacy of foreign policy" is antidemocratic because it presumes a "national interest" defined and guarded by an elite not beholden to the normal democratic contest.

Finally, the principles of democracy do not mesh too well with those of diplomacy. Diplomacy must be subtle; democracy lives by the rough and tumble of domestic politics. Democratic politics is to choose between stark alternatives, either ideological or personal; diplomacy is a game of ambiguous rules and stark dilemmas that are not so much resolved as muted or suspended. Democracy obeys the rule of law; diplomacy is the art of ruse and reinsurance. Democratic politics thrives on publicity and public discourse. Diplomacy must act with circumspection and secrecy, frequently pretending one objective (portrayed as lofty) even as it pursues another (which happens to be quite self-serving).

In short, democracies do not like Clausewitz. It is either total peace or total war, be it hot or cold. If suitably galvanized by an ideological threat and moral purpose, they will "pay any price" and "bear any burden," as John F. Kennedy put it, but they will not move smoothly along the "Clausewitzian continuum" where ideology means little and power everything, where diplomacy and force are but shades of one and the same spectrum of choices.

Yet if the Cold War (a.k.a. the ideological threat) is over, then we have a problem. Neo-isolationists could point to the collapse of Soviet power, declare victory, and go home. Internationalists could point to the collapse of communism, declare the "end of history," and also join the homeward trek. Both sides would unite in the conviction that America no longer needs to sustain the struggle—indeed, remain chained to the world—because the threat had vanished. Isolationists would feel safe in physical insulation; internationalists would conclude that the vision of the Enlightenment had at last come true. Since only despots make war, while democracies are inherently pacific, international politics henceforth will be reduced to global domestic policy. Welfare, not warfare, will shape its rules; global threats like ozone holes and pollution will dictate the agenda—and cooperation, to boot.

Realpolitikers ignore the domestic side of democratic foreign policy and pooh-pooh change. Idealpolitikers fall for the opposite temptation. Believing, as had Jefferson, that there is "but one system of ethics for men and for nations," they are always quick to spot a new "paradigm" in the making while ignoring that states, no matter what their constitution, remain chained to the self-help system. Whereas the citizen can *assume* security, the state cannot. In the self-help system, great conflicts like the Cold War may abate, even vanish—but not so the necessity to worry about security, status, and position. Old conflicts might return, new conflicts might supersede them. Even in peace, nations cannot take tranquility for granted as long as they live in a "state of nature" lacking both an arbiter of conflict and enforcer of peace.

The existence of *states* defines the essence of the game. Whence it follows that only their disappearance could usher in a new paradigm of global politics. Yet despite the onslaught of trans-, sub-, and supranational forces, the nation-state is alive and well. And so, the old rules of the self-help system will survive, too. Nor do the retraction of Soviet power and the collapse of Soviet ideology change the fundamentals. Even without its far-flung empire, Russia will still be the largest country on earth. Even with a democratic political culture, nuclear-armed Russia will still be the only country that can annihilate the United States.

Has nothing changed then? This is not the real issue. If completed, the democratization of the Soviet Union certainly would remove the peculiar intensity that attended the conflict in decades past. If continued, the retraction of Soviet power will remove many sources of the struggle—above all in Europe, the original and foremost arena of the Cold War, where the forward projection of Soviet power was the *casus belli*. Yet waning stridency and diminishing stakes do not signify the end of conflict, let alone the end of the self-help system. And so, there is no exit for the United States.

First, take the Soviet Union. Though lily-white democrats they might yet become, the heirs of Lenin and Stalin will still preside over the greatest military power apart from the United States. Though the competition will be muted and encased by cooperation, one thing will and cannot change: Unless the USSR self-destructs or another super-power arises, only America and Russia can extinguish each other. That is an existential fact with consequences. It limits both trust and cooperation, and it will keep the game of containment and counter-containment going. Each must still keep a wary eye on the other, and each must take care that his competitor-partner does not accumulate too many assets that might yet be turned to malign uses. And so, American policy must still harken the commands of the self-help system, cooperating where it can and competing where it must.

Second, take the international system. Twenty years after the first wave of "multipolarism," whose proponents declared the death of bipolarity and the birth of a tri- or quintapolar world, there is now the sequel with the subtitle "The Decline of American Power." The obvious need not be gainsaid. The United States is good merely for a quarter of the gross global product, and no longer for one-half. Germany (plus the EC) and Japan are serious, though still much smaller, commercial competitors, and there are at least five nuclear powers. As force has become less fungible, other "currencies" of influence have moved to the fore; power in general has become more diffused. Yet in a critical respect, the world is more "unipolar" than ever.

As was true twenty years ago, the United States is the only nation present at each gaming table—the strategic, the conventional military, the diplomatic, economic, and ideological-cultural. And at each table, it is the dominant player to boot. The Soviet Union was always a developing country with thermonuclear weapons; today, it is an economic basket case which has lost even its ideological trump card. To make this case is not to crow but to stress the special responsibility that has devolved upon America as its existential rival is deflating.

Nor are the new centers of power—Germany, Japan, China—ready to assume the burden of global management. China is a societal earthquake waiting to happen. Germany has its hands full with reunification and thereafter will be busy with its many conflicting obligations between EC integration and *Mitteleuropa,* between pacifying and containing Russia. Japan will have to come to grips with the sharpening tensions between consumerism and mega-mercantilism before even beginning to contemplate an autonomous strategic role in East Asia. The mighty yen and deutschemark can always bring down the American dollar, beholden as it is to the German interest rate and to Japanese bond hoarders. But neither Japan's Ministry of International Trade and Industry nor the Bundesbank can deal with Soviet SS–24 missiles, Lithuanian separatists, or Iraqi poison gas.

Which brings us to the third reason why there is no exit for the United States. As the previous dominant conflict (a.k.a. the Cold War) is declining, many lesser ones (with a heavy growth potential) are jostling to take the Cold War's place. Here is an abbreviated checklist: the disintegration of the Soviet Union, Iraqi ambitions, Libyan mischief, economic catastrophe in Eastern Europe, Yugoslavia's explosion, Arab–Israeli war, nuclear and poison-gas proliferation, Islamic fundamentalism, the collapse of the marvelous Western economy that stretches from Frankfurt via New York to Tokyo. Take your pick and try to imagine any crisis management minus the United States.

To all of this, a neo-isolationist might rightfully reply: "You have made the *world's* case for America's entanglement. But what's in it for the *United States?*" The point is well taken. To shoulder the burden would require a sense of responsibility that is costly and not self-evident to a society unwilling to sustain *les vastes entreprises* (as de Gaulle put it) in the absence of an overweening ideological threat. Moreover, many items on the checklist of conflict do not undermine the isolationist creed because such crises do not necessarily affect American physical security. Let the Europeans take care of Qaddafi. Yugoslavia '90 is not Sarajevo '14; today, no great power will start World War III because of Serbian nationalism.

The counterreply is an old one. If you don't believe that power is destiny, then how about: "What is good for the world is good for America?" While it is true that a nuclear-armed United States can assure its own security (as it always could), great powers have interests which transcend their national space, requiring order beyond borders. Conflict in Yugoslavia may not spill over; conflict in the Middle East, a strategic locale harboring a strategic resource (oil), has a nasty habit of attracting outsiders. Europe may be on the road to pacification, but it is not foreordained that the Continent can take care of itself.

The underlying problem has hardly vanished. There is Russia, larger and militarily more potent than anybody else, and there is Germany, the biggest economic player at the fulcrum of the European balance which is now being liberated from the fetters of dependence the Cold War has wrought. On the other hand, there is an abiding American interest in European order for reasons both strategic and economic (which this analysis assumes to be self-evident). If the past 120 years are a guide, Germany and Russia are not the ideal comanagers. When they have not been at each other's throat, they have conspired against the rest while simultaneously trying to weaken each other. By contrast,

Europe has flourished, as after 1945, when a power stronger than both was ensconced in the system. That power was, and remains, America.

The United States need not be there with 300,000 troops once force levels come down everywhere. But given America's stake in a prosperous and peaceful Europe, the United States ought to play the same role tomorrow as it did yesterday: as protector and pacifier from within. America on the inside would hold the balance against a diminished, but still potent Soviet Union. And in so doing, the United States would pull the sting of German power, thus allowing the entire continent to acquire the cooperative habits that came to bless Western Europe in the past forty years. It should not be assumed that an autochthonous order will arise, just because the Cold War structures are crumbling. Renationalization and the return to pre-1945 modes of behavior are just as likely in the absence of an Atlantic anchor.

But what if there is a "new paradigm" in the making—with welfare shouldering aside warfare? That would add, rather than subtract, reasons for America living up to its Number One role. Twenty years ago, exports came to 4 percent of American GNP; today, that proportion has more than doubled. At the same time, America's vulnerability to global economic forces (interest rates, capital movements, protectionism) has soared. While the United States can no longer dominate the world economy, its two closest competitors (Germany–EC and Japan) are neither willing nor able to assume the burden of global management that underlies the marvelous resilience of the Western economy. By virtue of size and position, the United States remains the hub. That role and new vulnerabilities hardly counsel self-sufficiency because the United States will suffer more than most if free trade and monetary stability collapse. But there is more: Precisely because the United States has accumulated new economic handicaps in the 1970s and 1980s, it must not abandon its politico-strategic assets. Being present in Europe, for instance, gives the United States a more audible say in economic decision-making than from a solitary perch across the Atlantic.

Granted, but why should Washington bomb Qaddafi, stop Iraqi nuclear ambitions, fiddle with Messrs. Shamir and Arafat, "resocialize" Iran, democratize Nicaragua, and seek a settlement in Cambodia? The answer is twofold. First, while peace and the "new paradigm" might yet rule over the "northern" world that stretches eastward from San Francisco to Vladivostok, the "old paradigm"—ambition, fear, and violence—is alive and well everywhere else. Second, these conflicts have a way of impinging on the United States. Iraqi nuclear weapons may pose threats at one step removed, but when Pan Am 103 explodes over Lockerbie, the challenge is direct, brutal, and bloody.

Wherever the "old paradigm" persists, American interests will be affected. Nor could American interests be scaled down like those, say, of Canada, in order to get out of harm's way. The United States is too big, too visible, and too much of a weight in the balance to revert to the role Tocqueville had described thus: "The country is as much removed from the passions of the Old World by its position as by its wishes, and it is called upon neither to repudiate nor to espouse them"; hence "the foreign policy of the United States . . . consists more in abstaining than in acting." Yet today, even abstention will have consequences for the world and then for America itself, and so there is no exit.

Finally, there is also *pleasure* in being Number One. To exert power is better than suffering it; to be at the helm is better than hunkering down in the hold. With the Soviet Union (temporarily) receding from the world scene, the United States need not respond to each and every change by treating it as harbinger of bigger and worse things to come. There will be some safety in indifference, and not every crisis need be approached as if it were a wholly owned subsidiary of American diplomacy. But the death of communism spells neither the birth of a new order nor the end of conflict. It is the great powers that build and maintain international order, and those who shape it most also gain most. With the decline of the Soviet Union, there is only one truly great power left in the system. Therein lies the purpose and the profit of American power at the threshold of the twenty-first century.

16

A NORMAL COUNTRY IN A NORMAL TIME

JEANE J. KIRKPATRICK

It is the first time since 1939 that there has been an opportunity for Americans to consider what we might do in a world less constrained by political and military competition with a dangerous adversary. The United States arrives at the end of the Cold War with some obvious assets. We are a powerful, affluent country with real strengths, great but limited resources, some bad habits, and a few real problems. We have virtually no experience in protecting and serving our interests in a multipolar world in which diverse nations and groups of nations engage in an endless competition for marginal advantages. This is precisely the kind of world now taking shape.

Assuming our resources and their limits—what kinds of goals should Americans and the U.S. government pursue in this post–Cold War period in which there is no pressing need for heroism and sacrifice? Some preliminary observations should help in answering the question.

American purposes are mainly domestic. A good society is defined not by its foreign policy but by its internal qualities—by the existence of democracy, opportunity, fairness; by the relations among its citizens, the kind of character nurtured, and the quality of life lived.

Foreign policy becomes a major aspect of a society only if its government is expansionist, imperial, aggressive, or when it is threatened by aggression. One of the most important consequences of the half century of war and Cold War has been to give foreign affairs an unnatural importance. The end of the Cold War frees time, attention, and resources for American needs.

America's chief collective purpose should be to make a good society better: more productive, more cohesive, more caring, more safe, more challenging, more serious.

Our purposes in the world are merely human, not transcendental. Unlike countries with a long complex history and a clear national composition, the United States is the quintessential eighteenth-century contractarian society—a people who constituted themselves by political will, who defined themselves in terms of their purposes and organized a government—all much as John Locke described. The U.S. Constitution is the act of incorporation whose preamble defines and limits our collective purposes. Only one of the purposes stated there unambiguously applies to foreign affairs: to "provide for the common defense."

There is no mystical American "mission" or purpose to be "found" independently of the U.S. Constitution and government. There is no inherent or historical "imperative" for the U.S. government to seek to achieve any other goal—

however great—except as it is mandated by the Constitution and adopted by the people through elected officials.

To be legitimate, the American government's purposes must be ratified by popular majorities. Except in the case of urgent, unanticipated events of great importance, the U.S. government cannot legitimately devote taxpayer monies to any cause not authorized by democratically elected officials—not to the establishment of democracy around the world, nor the elimination of war, hunger, and chaos, nor the establishment of a stable world order, nor an orderly global trading system, nor any other worthy good *except* as these issues are discussed and endorsed by majorities of voters and adopted by their elected representatives. It can be expected that policies so adopted will reflect U.S. national character and basic values.

It is frequently argued that foreign policy is so different from domestic policy that majority rule should not apply. It is certainly true that foreign policy has distinctive characteristics. Its objects are more remote and exotic than the objects of domestic politics. Because most people know less about foreign than domestic affairs, the issues can more readily be distorted and manipulated. And as Tocqueville noted, the common sense and everyday experience of ordinary people is less readily relevant. It is also true that foreign policy decisions may be uniquely catastrophic. Major mistakes in economic policy may cost people their jobs and income, but major mistakes in foreign policy cost people their freedom and their lives.

Under the conditions of global interdependence and proliferating weapons of mass destruction, U.S. foreign policy has become progressively complicated, expensive, and dangerous. More nations, more civilizations, more horrors are involved. American civilians—like the passengers on the

Achille Lauro—have been sucked into foreign affairs in new ways as the United States became involved with countries and people who consider us all combatants in an ongoing war for the liberation of somewhere.

It has become more important than ever that the experts who conduct foreign policy on our behalf be subject to the direction and control of the people. We should reject utterly any claim that foreign policy is the special province of special people—beyond the control of those who must pay its costs and bear its consequences.

Like many other aspects of social policy, foreign affairs requires expert knowledge from those who frame issues and options and implement policies. But this is no reason to exempt it from democratic controls.

Only elected officials, continuously reminded of their immediate dependence on the people, can insure that government does not impose inappropriate, excessive, or unbearable demands on the polity. Elected officials must therefore accept responsibility for foreign policy, and we the people should hold them responsible for its conduct. This means that discussion of the broad issues of foreign policy should have an important place in any election campaign. Such discussion is not the rowdy intrusion often charged; it is an essential element of democratic government in an interdependent world.

Foreign policy elites may have distinctive views. Maintaining popular control of foreign policy is especially important because foreign policy elites often have different views than those of popular majorities. In the long years of World War II and the Cold War, the United States developed a foreign policy elite based in the bureaucracy, academic institutions, and heavily associated with nonprofit institutions. Members of this foreign policy elite grew accustomed to thinking of the United States as having boundless resources and purposes which transcended the preferences of voters and apparent American interests— expansive, expensive, global purposes—and eventually developed a disinterested globalist attitude which became identified with the liberal position in foreign policy.

In American discussions of foreign policy, "internationalism" is often identified with this "disinterested globalism," and opposition to it is thought of as "isolationism." But disinterested globalism is only one American variant of internationalism, rarely practiced by other governments, most of which practice another variety of internationalism.

As for isolationism, most Americans know it is not a viable alternative in the contemporary world. The isolationism versus internationalism debate is in reality the debate among the various *types* of internationalism: that which aims frankly to serve the national interest, as conventionally conceived (to protect its territory, wealth, and access to necessary goods; to defend its nationals); that which aims to preserve and defend democracy; and a brand of "disinterested globalism" which looks at the world and asks what needs to be done—with little explicit concern for the national interest.

Today, when the Soviet Union has lost its political dynamism, when democracy is growing in strength, when Europe, Japan, Taiwan, Korea are strong and friendly, the United States is free to focus again on its own national interests without endangering the civilization of which it is a part. That is a normal condition for nations. It is not incompatible with playing a constructive global role.

What should we do? The United States should first clean up the residue of the Cold War and the communist threat: eliminating Soviet troops and weapons from Eastern Europe, negotiating the dramatic reduction of strategic weapons, drawing down American forces and commitments overseas, and assuming no new obligations in remote places.

There are two new major tasks which U.S. foreign policy should address. It should support the U.S. economy and work to strengthen democracy.

First, the U.S. government has the responsibility for writing and negotiating rules under which American business can compete effectively internationally. It is the U.S. government's responsibility to negotiate rules which give U.S. products fair access to foreign markets and give foreign businesses no better than fair access to U.S. markets; to make certain that U.S. laws (such as antitrust laws) do not handicap U.S. industry in competing with European and Asian firms; to ensure that the patterns of trade competition do not undermine the United States' industrial and technological base; to provide a strong, stable dollar that does not handicap American businesses seeking to deal in foreign environments and does not give foreign competitors an advantage in acquiring resources on the American and international markets. This is a *government* responsibility that cannot be ignored because of anxieties about an "industrial" policy.

Second, while it is not the American purpose to establish "universal dominance," in the provocative formulation of Charles Krauthammer—not even the universal dominance of democracy—it is enormously desirable for the United States and others to encourage democratic institutions wherever possible. Democratic institutions are not only the best guarantee that a government will respect the rights of its citizens, they are the best guarantee that a country will not engage in aggressive wars. Democratic institutions are the best arms control plan, the best peace plan for any area. A democratic Soviet government would quickly resolve outstanding problems in negotiating verifiable, mutual arms reductions. Democratic governments in the Middle East would resolve the so-called Arab–Israeli problem.

It is not within the United States' power to democratize the world, but we can and should make clear our views about the consequences of freedom and unfreedom. We can and should encourage others to adopt democratic practices.

What we should not do. A decent regard for the interests of American taxpayers and national interests also indicates that there are some things the U.S. government should not do.

The United States should not seek to manage the political evolution of the Soviet Union. It is a large, sovereign country, very different from our own, with whom we have no special influence, and in which we have no special interest (except as a military threat). There are several reasons we should not offer significant financial aid.

We should not imagine that we can "save" Gorbachev, either with massive economic aid or any other way, because his tenure will depend on internal political factors beyond our control.

Economic aid will not necessarily help the Soviet economy out of its current crisis. Almost everyone understands that the sweeping structural changes required for the Soviet economy to grow have been slow in coming. So has the needed reorientation of incentives. Americans do not know at this stage what is best for the Soviet people. Who would be more likely to move the peoples of the Soviet Union toward self-government and self-determination? Who would be more likely to provide self-determination to the constituent "republics" of the Soviet Union seeking autonomy? Who would be more likely to remove Soviet troops from Eastern Europe? Who would be more likely to reduce and destroy arms?

Any notion that the United States can manage the changes in that huge, multinational, developing society is grandiose. It is precisely the kind of thinking about foreign policy which Americans need to unlearn. We should also not get nervous, but understand that a period of instability in Eastern Europe is a necessary price of freedom for those long-suffering people.

The United States should also not try to manage the balance of power in Europe—we should neither seek to prevent nor assist Germany in reestablishing a dominant position in Europe or in Central Europe. We could not control these matters if we tried, and there is no reason to try. A united *democratic* Germany is a threat to no one. There have been forty years for the United States and Western democracies to encourage democratic political culture and institutions. There have been decades of careful, step-by-step movement toward a European Community and Atlantic Alliance, one of whose functions is to integrate and reinforce democratic institutions of member states. If those have not accomplished the task, there is not much we can do now. The United States also cannot eliminate the anxieties of Germany's neighbors—only positive experience with a powerful, sovereign Germany can do that. Neither can the United States be expected to sustain an expensive role in an alliance whose chief role is to diminish European fear of a resurgent Germany. Americans have more pressing priorities.

The relative strength and weight within Europe of the various European countries will be settled—peacefully, one trusts—by European countries in European arenas in which the United States will have a small role. This should be regarded by Americans as liberating rather than depriving the United States.

The United States should also not seek to balance power between Japan, China, and, say, India, in North or South Asia; nor try to contain Japan's role in Asia and in the world. Our concern with Japan should above all be with its trading practices with the United States. We should not spend American money protecting an affluent Japan, though a continuing alliance with Japan is entirely appropriate.

A normal country in a normal time. The United States performed heroically in a time when heroism was required; altruistically during the long years when freedom was endangered.

The time when Americans should bear such unusual burdens is past. With a return to "normal" times, we can again become a normal nation—and take care of pressing problems of education, family, industry, and technology. We can be an independent nation in a world of independent nations.

Most of the international military obligations that we assumed were once important are now outdated. Our alliances should be alliances of equals, with equal risks, burdens, and responsibilities. It is time to give up the dubious benefits of superpower status and become again a usually successful, open American republic.

This is, in any case, the American purpose today—as I understand it. I believe these views are broadly shared by the majority of Americans.

Should that not be the case, I would, of course, respect their decision.

INDEX

CONTRIBUTORS

Robert L. Bartley is editor of the *Wall Street Journal.*

Patrick J. Buchanan, a former presidential assistant to Richard Nixon and Ronald Reagan, is a syndicated columnist and a nightly commentator on Cable News Network.

Ted Galen Carpenter is director of foreign policy studies at the Cato Institute in Washington, D.C.

Carl Gershman is president of the National Endowment for Democracy.

Owen Harries is the editor of the *National Interest.*

Nathan Glazer is professor of education and sociology at Harvard University.

Josef Joffe is foreign editor and columnist of the *Süddeutsche Zeitung* in Munich, and is the Beaton Michael Kenab Professor of National Security Affairs at Harvard University in 1990–91.

Jeane J. Kirkpatrick is former U.S. ambassador to the United Nations. She is currently a senior fellow at the American Enterprise Institute and Leavey Professor at Georgetown University.

Charles Krauthammer is a syndicated columnist.

Irving Kristol is publisher of the *National Interest* and a distinguished fellow at the American Enterprise Institute.

Stephen J. Solarz is a Democratic representative from New York.

Nathan Tarcov is associate professor of political science at the University of Chicago. He was a member of the State Department's Policy Planning Staff from 1981 to 1982.

Michael Vlahos is director of the State Department's Center for the Study of Foreign Affairs. The views expressed are those of the author and do not necessarily reflect those of the U.S. government.

Malcolm Wallop is a Republican senator from Wyoming.

Ben J. Wattenberg is a senior fellow at the American Enterprise Institute and vice chairman of the board of Radio Free Europe and Radio Liberty.

Paul M. Weyrich is president of the Free Congress Foundation.

Peregrine Worsthorne is editorial page editor of the *London Sunday Telegraph.*

Designed by David Peattie
in Adobe Garamond

Indexed by Shirley Kessel

Printed by R. R. Donnelley & Sons
Harrisonburg, Virginia